K. DOUGLAS

LIFE AROUND US

LIFE AROUND US

by Howard F. King
formerly Head of Biology Department
Grammar School for Boys, Cambridge

Illustrated by Josephine Marquand

Heinemann Educational Books Ltd
London

Heinemann Educational Books Ltd
London Melbourne Toronto Johannesburg
Singapore Auckland Ibadan
Hong Kong Nairobi

SBN 435 59090 1

First published 1969

Published by Heinemann Educational Books Ltd
48 Charles Street, London W.1.
Printed by Latimer Trend & Co. Ltd.
Whitstable

Preface

This book arises from the author's own struggle to achieve certain objectives in biology teaching to secondary school pupils. These objectives may be indicated under three broad headings: to build an understanding of the workings of the pupil's own body, to portray the range of life forms, their origin and continuance, and to show biology as a scientific study, working from the evidence provided by observation and experiment.

We cannot do everything at once, and not all these objectives can be pursued to an equal extent in the first year or two. Accordingly, this course of study deals with the activities characteristic of life, and the range of living things, but contains very little on the structure and functions of the human body. Emphasis is placed throughout on direct observation and experiment, and on finding answers for oneself. An attempt has been made to avoid giving information which the pupil can reasonably find out for himself. In this way one hopes to promote a scientific attitude, however disconcerting such an approach may be to those pupils who much prefer, or are accustomed to, having their information just handed out! This method may at times prove more difficult for the pupil than the habit of using experiments and other practical work to illustrate what has already been stated. It is, however, more stimulating for the pupil and the teacher, and I think in the end more rewarding for both. Although apparatus is required quite often, it is of simple construction and of common laboratory items. The course is planned on a basis of a single period a week in the first year, and two periods per week in the second year. Provided the teacher will take it at appropriate pace, select where necessary, and adjust the amount of help he gives to the pupils, the course should provide suitable for a wide variety of classes.

Stress is laid on accuracy of work, and on the written recording of what has been done. This is justifiable, if justification is needed, not because it produces a neat notebook or a convenient means of rote learning, but because it aids the pupil's comprehension of what has been done and why. In other words, as an aid to the appreciation of the logical structure of science.

However much attention we give to individual organisms in the classroom or the laboratory, we have an incomplete picture of their biology unless we consider their part in their native community. Field work has its place in this scheme of work, which is so arranged that the sections on collecting organisms for freshwater aquaria and on the hedgerow can be tackled in the summer terms of the first and second years. In addition, the chapter on winter survival is related to hedgerow and roadside organisms.

H. F. K.

Contents

Acknowledgments

The pupils of the Grammar School for Boys, Cambridge, were the test population on which this course was tried out, not all at once, but part by part as it grew out of their work. Their responses, sometimes favourable, sometimes otherwise, have much to do with some items being in the book, and others excluded! My thanks are due to them for the way in which their enthusiasm has encouraged me over several years. The lively ideas and forward-looking teaching of my colleagues in the Science Department at that school contributed much to the development of my own thought. I have had many stimulating discussions on the teaching of biology with Mr E. F. Holden, Senior Science Master, the Cambridgeshire High School for Boys.

The photographs for Figure 38 were taken by Mr A. E. C. George, of the Grammar School for Boys, Cambridge. The slide of Azotobacter for Figure 40 was provided by Mr G. Elis Jones, the Honorary Treasurer of the Society for Applied Bacteriology.

Figures $31(f)$, 50, $58(b)$, $59(b)$, $60(a)$, 70, $75(b)$ and $82(c)$ are reproduced by kind permission of the Radio Times Hulton Picture Library. The Frontispiece is reproduced by kind permission of the Trustees of the British Museum (Natural History). The photographs reproduced as figures 5, 18, $31(a)$, $31(e)$, $32(a)$, $32(b)$, $32(c)$, $47(a)$, (b) & (c), $49(b)$, $51(a)$, (b), $53(d)$, $55(a)$, $57(a)$ & (b), $58(a)$, $59(a)$, $60(b)$, $60(c)$, $62(a)$, 67, $68(a)$, $69(a)$, (b), (c), 71, 72, $74(c)$, (d), (e), 78, $82(a)$ were taken by Mr Chan Kwok Hoi. Figure 6 is reproduced by kind permission of Dr E. V. Watson and Cambridge University Press.

Mr L. C. Comber and Mr C. D. Bingham read through the manuscript and I am much indebted to them for the many valuable suggestions they made. Needless to say, the faults of the work are all my own. Mr Hamish MacGibbon, the Science Director of Heinemann Educational Books Ltd, has been a constant source of help and encouragement throughout the book's preparation. Above all, it could not have been completed without the patient tolerance, as well as the practical help, of my wife and family.

One

The science of biology

Life on Earth

A vast swirling mass of gas and dust slowly began to take on a more definite, solid form and Earth was born, some 4,500 million years ago, a part of the immense Universe. The study of that Universe we call astronomy, one of the oldest fields of man's attempts to come to an understanding of his surroundings. In the Universe we observe electrical discharges, light, heat, sound; the study and the measurement of these is the province of physics.

As the centre of Earth's mass slowly turned to a more solid state it became a lumpy mixture made up of, in the main, the metals iron and nickel, and the non-metals sulphur and silicon, with many other substances in lesser amounts. In the course of time the solid matter of Earth developed, as we believe, its present molten core and surrounding mantle of rock, with the very thin layer of crust which supports all life. In that crust are to be found many different materials, 'chemicals', the study of whose behaviour and reactions is chemistry.

But the Earth, having formed, was not unchanging; great upheavals from below thrust up prominences, the mountains, and produced hollows which became filled with water, the seas. Yet even now all was not still for the effects of heat and frost, rain and ice, gradually wore away, as they still do, the rocks already exposed. Fragments of rock were carried down in streams and rivers, to be deposited elsewhere, creating new scenery. Here is the field of geography, with its study of Earth and its features, and the way that man's life and his industries relate to them; and of geology, concerned with the structure of the rocks and the ways of their formation.

And what of living things? The earliest traces of what was once life, in the shape of preserved remains (fossils), are dated back 500 million years or more. Some such fossils show kinship to plants or animals of the present world; others bear little such resemblance. Even so, the oldest traces we have found of living things show us signs of well-developed, complicated bodies, and we can only guess at the nature of still earlier forms. The groups of living things which play a dominating part on the land today, the flowering plants and mammals, were not present then; their history is a more recent one, although still to be measured in many millions of years. Man himself occupies only the last few lines of the book of life, a mere million years or so, and his recorded history only a few thousand years. Here archaeology merges into history, and the great mental development of the human kind gives rise to all our other studies, languages and mathematics, as well as music and art. But although man becomes a scholar, he still remains a living creature, a part of the great community of life which is the subject-matter of biology. The name comes from the Greek words *bios*—life, and *logos*—knowledge.

There are about two million different kinds of animals and plants in existence on Earth today, and the living substance of which they are made (protoplasm) proves to be tremendously complex. There is here a fascinating and limitless opportunity for intelligent enquiry and investigation, and it is not too soon for you to begin.

'Why study biology?' The keen biologist may well dismiss such a question with contempt; he finds it, or his own particular branch of that subject, so fascinating that he can hardly imagine anyone wanting a reason! Yet there are many sound reasons why everyone should grasp some of the knowledge and ideas of biology; it is so important to the welfare of Man himself.

The human body is one important object of biological study. Everyone ought to know at least the broad outlines of how his own body works, and how its various functions are carried out, so that he can use all his powers wisely and well. Even so, there will be times when the body becomes weakened by illness or disease; it is then that modern medicine based on biological knowledge, comes to his aid. He staggers to bed with a headache and a rising temperature; in comes the doctor, diagnoses the illness as a throat infection, and gives an 'antibiotic'. Soon he is on his feet again. He had been attacked by living organisms, bacteria, so small as to need a powerful microscope to see them at all, but whose way of life has been carefully worked out by biologists. These bacteria had multiplied in his throat faster than the body's own defences could kill them off. To get rid of them, the product of other living things, this time a kind of mould, discovered by other biologists, had been collected, purified and made into tablets.

Every year there are more people on Earth than there have ever been before. Many of them will go desperately hungry, or die at a very early age, because their countries do not produce, and cannot afford to buy, sufficient food for them. The Food and Agriculture Organisation of the United Nations seeks to teach such people ways of growing more food by using new crops, or better varieties of the usual crops, by new methods of cultivation, by better use of the available land, and by bringing into farming what were previously wild areas. Wherever food crops are grown, there is a great host of animal pests waiting for free meals – such as greenfly sucking plant juices, locusts eating leaves, stem and all, or weevils chewing their way through stored grain. To combat them demands further knowledge, other skills. Here again the biologist must provide the information on when and how to defeat the pests' attack.

So one might go on – combat of disease, safeguarding water supplies, ensuring the purity of food, and so on – all powerful reasons for encouraging the study of biology. Nevertheless, I think you will find that the most important reason of all is that the story of life is a fascinating and immensely enjoyable pursuit.

The Methods of Biology

How shall we tackle our subject? Biology is a science. This means that biologists use the same methods as other scientists (see Fig. 1). Science begins with *observation*, as when we watch under a microscope blood flowing through the webbed foot of a frog or count how many plants have grown from the hundred pea seeds we planted. At this point, science has a good deal in common with detective work; the great investigator in the crime story goes round the room, noticing this and that clue, while his friends and assistants gasp at his prowess! Correct investigation is something we must learn, to make the most of what our eyes, our noses and our sense of touch can tell us. If we make errors at this stage, or fail to spot something which may be a little unusual or unexpected, then the chance of making a contribution to science is lost.

Our observations lead us to ask *questions*, such as 'How does the frog send blood round its body?' or 'What was the reason for ten of the pea seeds failing to grow?' More than one

3

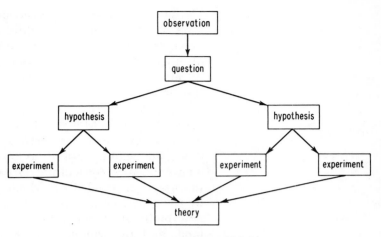

Fig. 1 Methods of biology

answer may be possible from the evidence we have available, although often we may have a shrewd suspicion as to which one is likely to be correct,

For example, you are riding your bicycle when you are dismayed to find that the front tyre is becoming flat. This might be due to a leaky valve, to the inner-tube being old so that air is slowly escaping from many places, or to the tube having been punctured. If, on examining it, you see a sharp stone embedded in the tyre, you would regard the last as the most likely! At this point the scientist will usually frame his answer in the form of a statement or *hypothesis*, the truth of which he can then put to the test. This is done by *experiment*. An experiment is a practical test specially designed to provide clear information about the correctness of such a hypothesis.

In our bicycle example, you could test your hypothesis that the stone had punctured the inner-tube by removing the tube and putting it in a bucket of water. If bubbles of air came from one particular place, this would be clear evidence supporting the hypothesis. Your next 'experiment' would be the sticking of a patch over the hole. If the tube no longer lost air, the hypothesis would be confirmed. Designing the right experiments is a skilled piece of work, and often takes far longer than actually doing them. We must practice this too.

If we are establishing a definite answer to our question, then we can propose a *theory*: 'The frog's blood is circulated by a heart, an organ which carries out a rapidly repeated pumping action.' Other biologists might wish to test our theory in their own laboratories, and by their own methods; if they agree with us, our theory will pass into the generally-accepted body of scientific knowledge. It may then be used to predict what will happen in other cases; for example, that a similar pump would be found in other animals with body structure like that of a frog, such as newts and salamanders. The example discussed has, of course, been well worked-over for many years. It was in the reign of King Charles I that Dr Harvey first demonstrated the circulation of blood round the human body by the pumping action of the heart, and later other biologists showed that similar blood systems occurred in other backboned animals.

There are still thousands of other problems needing answers to be found by careful observation of plants and animals, sometimes dead and dissected on the laboratory bench, but often alive in their native haunts. The painstaking observation of living things in their own territory is still one of the most profitable areas for new investigations, many of which can be carried out by the amateur no less than by the experienced professional biologist. There is still a tremendous number of things worth knowing to be discovered about the lives of our native British animals and plants. If this prospect interests you, have a good look at Alan Dale's book, *Observations and Experiments in Natural History*, published by Heinemann Educational Books. Meanwhile, we will begin our study of biology; I hope you will enjoy it.

In the previous chapter we considered the methods of science in relation to biology. This chapter presents a few investigations for you to carry out, and so put to use the scientific method. What you find out from these experiments may suggest to you further lines of enquiry.

Experiment 1. Collect a number of earwigs. They can be found in such places as hollow stems, in the heads of large flowers such as sunflowers or chrysanthemums, or hiding under dead leaves and stems lying on the earth. When you have half a dozen or so release them into an empty aquarium tank or a large empty box. What is the *first* thing noticeable? Where are they after an interval of two minutes?

Repeat the experiment – you can use the same earwigs – but this time, before releasing them, put into your tank a few dead leaves or small pieces of stick. Again observe the earwigs' behaviour.

What have you found out about earwigs? Try to work out ways in which you could follow up your ideas and test their correctness.

Write in your laboratory notebook a careful account of what you set out to do (aim), how you did it (method), what you observed (results), and then set down any conclusions which you consider justified. Remember that your account of method should be sufficient to enable another person to follow the exact procedure, but it should be kept as concise as possible. Often, a simple diagram saves many lines of writing.

Here is an example of a 'written-up' experiment:

Aim: To find if blowfly maggots respond to light.

Method: Six blowfly maggots were obtained* and placed under a dark box on the bench. A beam of light was shone into the box from one end, as shown in the diagram (see Fig. 2). When the response of the maggots had been observed, the light was moved to the opposite end and their behaviour again noticed.

Results: The maggots all crawled away from the source of light. When the light was moved to the other end, they reversed direction so that they were again crawling towards the darker end.

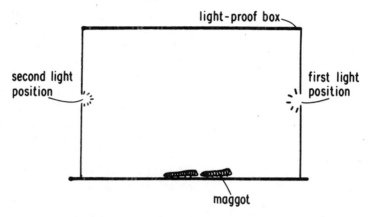

Fig. 2   Experiment on the response of maggots to light

Conclusion: Maggots can detect light. They move away from the source of light.

Notice the following points:

1.   The experiment has a definite object.

2.   The description is written in the *past tense* and in an impersonal way. This is the usual practice in scientific work, so we will follow it from the beginning.

3.   The method gives enough detail, with the aid of the diagram, to enable anyone wishing to check our results to repeat the experiment in exactly the same way.

4.   The conclusion must not go beyond what the results indicate. If we had written in the conclusion 'maggots have eyes' this would not be justified because there is no proof from the experiment that the light is detected by anything

---

* If you would like to try this experiment for yourself, you can obtain maggots from a fishing tackle shop.

recognisable as eyes. Nor does the experiment give us any information about the value to the maggot of its reaction to light, but a close study of the maggot's habits and mode of life might give the clue.

Experiment 2. The aim here is to study reproduction in an aphid. Aphids are small insects with a slender needle-like mouth apparatus which pierces the young stems and leaves of plants and then sucks the juices. Examples are the 'green-fly' found on roses, and on many potted plants, and the 'blackfly' which are sometimes found in great numbers on broad bean plants.

What parts of the plant does the aphid usually inhabit? Can you offer an explanation?

Now take a lightly-infested part of the plant, say a single shoot, and reduce the greenfly to just one survivor. Alternatively you may be able to dislodge one without injury, although this is not easy, and transfer it to an aphid-free shoot. Isolate the shoot in a larva cage, or a jam jar covered at the mouth with muslin, through which air can enter, with the base of the shoot dipping in water. Set up a second shoot, this time without any aphids, in exactly the same way. Examine daily for several days and count the number of greenfly visible. (If a number of people have done this experiment, collect all the totals and find the average number of offspring produced).

What have you learned about the greenfly's powers of producing more of its kind? Does it lay eggs? Might some of the greenfly have come from eggs that were too small to be seen easily? Your second shoot is a check on this. If the greenfly with which you began did not lay eggs, how did new aphids appear?

Experiment 3. For this you will need a single lump of horse dung collected while still quite fresh. Put it under a jar or other large glass container so as to prevent too much drying. Leave for a few days. The material provides food for more than one kind of mould (a mould is a plant belonging to the group known as Fungi), but soon the one in which we are presently interested, called *Pilobolus*, should appear. This is easily recognised by the shape of the sporangium or, as we may call it, the fruiting organ (see Fig. 3). This contains tiny round bodies called spores, each of which can under suitable conditions grow into a new plant. When the spores are ripe, the tube below the sporangium fills up with watery fluid until it suddenly bursts, propelling the sporangium upwards into the air, to fall some distance away; in our experiment the sporangia are likely to stick to the glass.

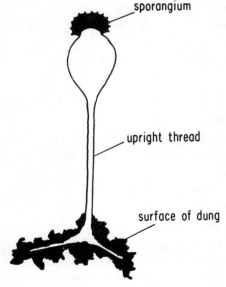

sporangium

upright thread

surface of dung

Fig. 3 *Pilobolus* fruiting body. The whole upright structure is less than 1 cm high

Find out if the direction in which the sporangium is propelled is related to the direction of most light. If two jars are used, one can be left exposed to the light on all sides, while the other can be covered with dark paper except for a small round hole on one side. About 10 days after setting up the experiment you will be able to compare the positions of the sporangia on the walls of the jars. Has light had any effect on the angle at which the sporangia have been discharged?

Experiment 4. Lastly, an experiment using seedlings of wheat or other grains. Soak about a dozen grains overnight, then leave them in a moist, warm place in the dark until the first shoot has grown to $\frac{1}{2}-\frac{3}{4}$ inch. Divide them into two equal batches. Keep one batch under a completely dark box, but put the other in a box which is dark except for a small window at one end. Leave for 1–2 days and then examine the shoots.

Have any of them grown straight up? Have any grown in a curve? If so, is this curve related to the position of the window?

These are just a tiny sample of the many interesting experiments which we can do; we shall be trying some more as we work through later chapters. These should be enough to show us the importance of careful method and accurate observation, and the full recording of both method and results if our work is to be of value. If these experiments have interested you, they may also have suggested further investigations to follow-up what you have found.

Three

On being alive

In the murder story (lots of them!) the great detective bent down to examine the victim and pronounced, with a shake of his head, 'He's dead'. What signs would he have looked for? You might suggest:

> No movement of any sort
> No sign of heart beat
> No breathing

for these are three quickly detectable activities which go on all the time we are alive. But what about those animals which have no heart to beat, such as a sea anemone, or plants, which don't seem either to move or to breathe? We can usually tell whether they are dead or alive! What does it really mean to say that something is 'alive'?

Think about yourself and your daily existence. How many different activities of your body can you distinguish? Perhaps your list would run like this:

> Eat
> Breathe
> Get rid of wastes
> Notice what's going on
> Move about
> Think
> Sleep

All the activities listed are part of our daily round, and some of them go on continually. Another is growth, which only occurs during the first part of our life. Eventually our bodies

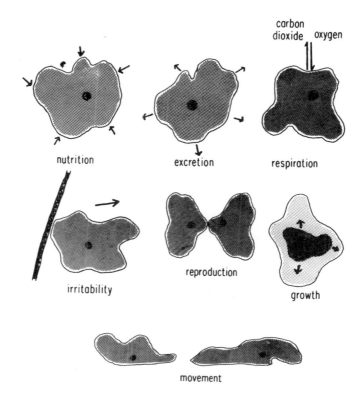

Fig. 4   The characteristic activities of living things, illustrated in
Amoeba (described in Chapter 13)

become worn out and we die, but long before that happens
most people have married and had children, so that the
human race continues. Which of the activities that we find
going on in our own life occur generally among living things?
Sleep may be ruled out – it is found only among a small
proportion of animals – and so can thinking, a term which
certainly cannot be applied to a plant!

The activities which do occur generally among living organisms are:

> Nutrition
> Respiration
> Excretion
> Irritability
> Growth
> Reproduction

Most animals are also capable of active movement (see
Fig. 4).

All living things are made up of a more-or-less fluid substance called *protoplasm*; in almost all living things except
some of microscopic size the protoplasm is divided into units
called *cells*.

Just as a vehicle will not run without fuel, so the living plant or animal requires food – food for providing energy (see below), or for building its body. This is what we mean by *nutrition*. Green plants are able to carry out the process of nutrition by making their own food from simple materials taken from the air and the soil. Animals take in complicated substances in the form of foods obtained from other animals, such as meat or milk, or from plants, as when we eat cabbage or bread. Animals must split up these elaborate materials into simpler ones, as when we digest our meals, before they can put them to use. We shall be taking a closer look at nutrition in a later chapter.

When a motor car engine is working, a series of sparks explode mixtures of petrol and the oxygen of air, and the energy so released makes the car go forward. But what do we mean by energy? Energy can be regarded as stored work. It can be used in many ways: the glowing of an electric light bulb, the heating of a kettle, the kicking of a ball, and the sending out of a wireless programme; all require an input of energy. Living things burn some of their food in order to release energy, but do it more slowly than the car burns its fuel. Some of the energy may be used in moving about, but much of it is needed to drive the body's internal processes. In ourselves, as in other mammals, and in birds, much energy is used in keeping our bodies constantly warm, even when the weather is very cold. The slow 'burning' of food inside the body to provide energy is what we mean by *respiration*, and to enable it to take place a supply of oxygen is required. The breathing movements we make help us to obtain enough oxygen for this purpose. We shall be having a further look at respiration at a later stage.

The processes which go on inside the body often result in the formation of useless substances – we could compare these to the exhaust fumes of the car – which might be harmful if allowed to pile up, so they undergo *excretion*. Excretion is the getting rid of waste substances produced during the body's various activities. One way in which waste is disposed of from our own bodies is the production of urine, and another, lesser way, is through sweat. In both these, waste substances are dissolved in water, among them the sodium chloride (the chemical name for common salt) which gives sweat its salty taste.

Experiment 5. To test for sodium chloride in human sweat.

One way of collecting a little sweat is to wear a rubber finger stall for a while – say, 15 minutes. If a platinum wire. one end of which is fixed in a holder, is rubbed in the sweat inside the finger stall and then held in a luminous bunsen

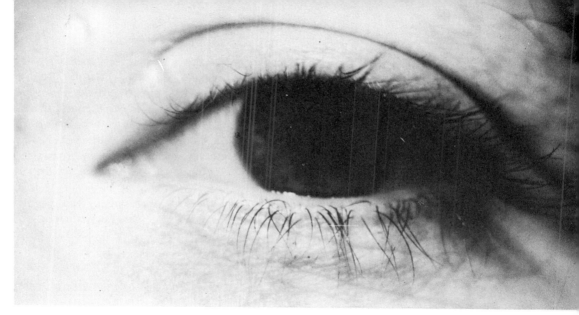

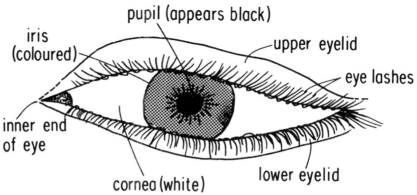

Fig. 5   Mirror view of human eye and diagram showing the
visible structures

flame, the flame is given a bright yellow colour. A pencil
shaped to give a long point will serve as a satisfactory sub-
stitute for the platinum wire, but take care not to set the
wood alight. Compare your result with that obtained when
the wire has been dipped in a solution of common salt dissolved in water. The colour obtained is that of the 'sodium
flame'. Now wash out the finger stall with a little pure (distilled) water, then add to the washings a few drops of silver
nitrate solution. Try this test also with common salt solution.
When silver nitrate solution is added to a solution of a
chloride, clouds of white substance, which remain when dilute
nitric acid is added, are formed .This is a standard chemical
test for 'chloride'. The white is silver chloride. Does the sweat
give the same result as common salt solution in each case?

Living things need to be aware of the outside world and
what is happening there, and to be able to respond in suitable

ways. This is what we mean by *irritability*. The experiments we carried out with earwigs, *Pilobolus*, and wheat seedlings all involved sensitivity to the outside world, and the last two remind us that plants have this capacity as well as animals, although they lack such structures as eyes and ears. Our own senses include sight, hearing, smell, taste and touch. Normally we use more than one sense at a time, as when our eyes and ears are used together in finding the source of a noise. The tremendous handicap which loss of one major sense causes, such as that due to blindness, can hardly be understood by those of us who have our full set of senses. Let us try two more experiments, this time on human senses.

Experiment 6. To find the effect of light and dark on pupil size.

Work with a partner. Put a hand over one eye so that the light is kept out, but be sure to keep both eyes open. After a couple of minutes, remove the hand and let your partner watch what happens. Do you notice any change in the size of the pupil (see Fig. 5)? If there was a change, did the pupil become smaller or larger? Would you describe the change as happening 'in a flash' or was it slow enough to be watched?

The iris, the coloured part of the eye, can alter the size of the pupil, through which light enters the eye, so that the delicate retina inside the eye which enables us to see shall not be damaged by too much light. Were you yourself aware of what was happening in your eye, or would you describe it as an unconscious action?

Experiment 7. To investigate the use of human senses in locating a sound.

Again, two people need to work together. If we hear a slight scratching sound, as of a pin against paper, the combined use of eyes and ears should enable us to detect its position almost at once. The second person should start timing with a stop-watch or the second hand of an ordinary watch when he begins to make the noise somewhere behind the first person's back. Take the time needed to put a finger on the point where the noise is being made. Now blindfold the first person, so he can make use of sound only. The experimenter should move to a new position, at about the same distance as previously, before scratching the paper again. Time as for the first trial. Try again with jobs reversed.

How do the times compare? Does the use of sound alone make no difference, only a small difference, or a large difference to the time required?

When an animal or plant begins its life it is small, but for a period of time it increases in size and weight; it shows *growth*. Plants generally go on growing slowly throughout their life, while most animals grow only for a time and stop at a certain age, by which time they are capable of producing more of their kind. Growth is too slow for us to watch it happening but here is a way of studying some aspects of growth in plants.

Experiment 8. To find out where growth occurs in a runner bean shoot.

Germinate a runner bean, or other large seed, by placing it in damp sand and leaving in a warm place for a week. It is important to position the bean correctly to get a straight shoot (see Fig. 6). When the shoot is 2–3 centimetres high make narrow lines 1 millimetre apart across the shoot, working downwards from the base of the folded leaves. This marking can be done by placing a strand of cotton, or thin wire, dipped in Indian ink, against the side of the shoot while this is lying against a ruler. Measure the total length of the shoot. When the ink is fully dry, put the seedling back in good conditions of moisture, warmth and light. Leave for two days.

What is the shoot length now? Look at the marks. Have all parts of the shoot grown equally? If not, where has most growth occurred?

Now here is something quite different to do, but still connected with growth. Table 1 gives the weight at various ages from birth of the four children of one family, as recorded

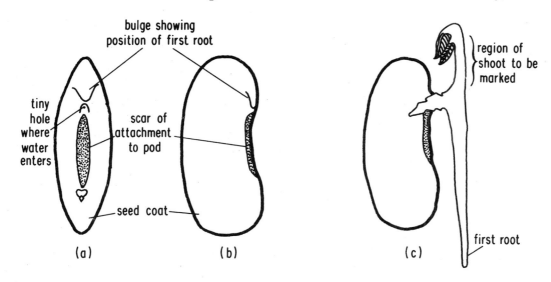

g. 6 Positioning a bean for measuring shoot growth. (*a*) Seed in end view. (*b*) The same seed seen
m a broad side. (*c*) The seedling ready for Experiment 8 after planting the seed the way up shown in
(*a*) and (*b*)

at an Infant Welfare Clinic. Plot these weights as a graph, using the horizontal scale for age in months and the vertical scale for weight. Use a different colour pencil for each child's set of figures. This will give us four 'growth curves'.

Table 1. Age and Weight of Four Children in a Family. The weights have been given to the nearest half-pound

Position in Family	Sex	Birth Weight		Age in Months							
			2	4	6	8	10	12	14	16	18
1	Girl	5 lb	9	13	15	17	18½	20	20	21	21½
2	Girl	6 lb	11	14	16	17½	19	19	20½	21½	21½
3	Boy	7½ lb	13	15½	17	19	20½	21½	23	24½	25½
4	Boy	6½ lb	12	14½	16½	18½	18½	20½	21½	22½	24½

Does weight increase occur at a more-or-less steady rate? If there are periods of no gain, or very little, can we suggest possible explanations? What do these results suggest about the comparative weights of infant boys and girls? Would it be fair to draw a definite conclusion on this point, using only these four sets of figures? What would you do to test your opinion?

The experiment you carried out earlier on aphids dealt with their *reproduction*, the capacity of living things to produce more of their own kind. Flowering plants do this through the production of seeds, fungi like *Pilobolus* produce spores, and many animals lay eggs, but mammals give birth to live young after the mother has nourished them inside her body for some time.

How many acorns on an oak tree in summer? Oak trees are known to live for a great many years, but when an oak dies, it will only be necessary for one of those acorns to have grown successfully to maintain the number of oaks. If an oak tree bears acorns for 100 years, and on average produces 500 acorns each summer, how many will it have borne by the end of its life? And how many of the acorns will need to grow into new trees to replace the parent? Many of the acorns are damaged before they fall from the tree. If you can get a number of acorns, cut or break them open and look for animals which have burrowed into the seed. Quite a few larger animals use acorns as food, too. What examples can you think of? Those acorns which do find their way into suitable ground may not be successful in producing new trees, for many seedlings are eaten off in their early stages of growth.

Not all living things bear large numbers of offspring; some produce a small number only, but give them protection, as a bird does when laying her shelled eggs, which she then incubates in a nest. Mammals, after protecting the young inside the mother's body, continue parental care after birth, and feed the young on milk. In these cases, few young are produced but there is a good chance of each one surviving to the age when it can reproduce.

Here are a number of organisms using various ways of reproduction (e.g. eggs, seeds).

Herring	Dogfish
Whale	Frog
Blackbird	Poppy
Mushroom	Fern
Pine	Garden Pea

Try to find out, where possible by direct investigation but otherwise by reference to books, the answers to the following questions:

How long does it live?

At what age does it begin to reproduce?

Does it reproduce on one occasion only, or on a number of separate occasions?

What is the method of reproduction?

What numbers of offspring are produced?

For our last point in this chapter, we come to take a look *inside* living things. We will start with some material taken from an onion.

Open an onion bulb, break off one of the fleshy scales which together form the bulk of the onion, and snap it crossways. You should now see pieces of delicate, almost transparent, skin on either side of the scale. Take a piece, say ¼ inch square, or smaller, and place it in a drop of water on a glass microscope slide. This can now be viewed under a microscope, after the mirror has been adjusted correctly for light (see Fig. 7).

You should view the slide with the lowest magnification first, since this is the best way of getting the object in the correct position. Focus the lens on to the object so as to get the clearest possible picture. On many microscopes focusing is by means of a milled knob, which may be on the tube itself or at the side. Wherever it is, the proper procedure is to *raise* the tube, i.e. to move the lens away from the object. If this means that the object gets further out of focus, it will be necessary to move the tube downwards while watching it from the side. This is *very important*; it ensures that the lens is not moved down to hit the glass microscope slide, which might well mean damage to an expensive lens.

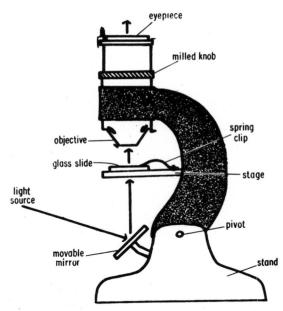

eyepiece

milled knob

objective

spring clip

glass slide

stage

light source

pivot

movable mirror

stand

Fig. 7 Diagram of a junior microscope. The pivot enables tilting of the microscope for more comfortable working, but care must be taken to avoid water draining from a glass slide onto the microscope. The light source can be daylight or a bench lamp. You will see two lenses, one in the eyepiece, the other in the objective. These must be kept clean with lens tissue

What do you see? Can you see a number of similar units, fitted together so as to give a continuous surface? Examine some of these units, the *cells*, to see as much detail as possible. The addition of a little iodine solution to the skin will help.

Can you distinguish something like a rim around the outside of the cell? This is the cell wall, and it is fairly rigid (see Fig. 8). Look also for other structures shown in Fig. 8; the *nucleus*, a roundish body which exerts a general control over the cell's working, and the large central space filled with clear fluid, the *vacuole*. Between the cell wall and the vacuole is the *cytoplasm*.

Now examine some other examples of plant cells, such as a very little tomato pulp spread out very, very thinly on a slide, or a slice of fresh beetroot or apple cut as thin as possible. Can you see the same features as in the cells from the onion skin?

To see some animal cells, gently scrape off a little of the inner lining of your cheek, using the *back* of a clean knife or similar instrument. Place the little collection of scrapings in a drop of water on a microscope slide, and examine them under the microscope. What similarities and differences from the onion cells do you notice?

Consider the size of the cells.

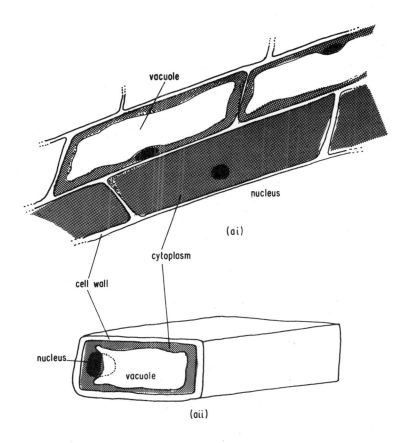

vacuole

nucleus

(ai)

cytoplasm

cell wall

nucleus

vacuole

(aii)

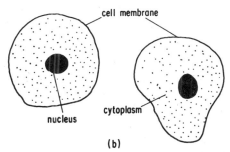

cell membrane

nucleus

cytoplasm

(b)

Fig. 8 (*ai*) Microscopic view of onion skin cells. (*aii*) Three-
dimensional veiw of one such cell with an end removed.
(*b*) Microscopic view of human cheek cells

Which have a cell wall, and which have only a very thin
outer boundary, the cell membrane?

Are vacuoles present in both, and if so are they of similar
proportion to total cell size?

Make simple, large size drawings to bring out these points
of comparison between the animal and plant cells.

In all organisms, apart from those of microscopic size, cells are present in very large numbers. In the human body there are something like a million million cells. Many of these cells are specially developed for particular functions, but all of them co-operate in the life of the body.

It has already been said that all living things are made up of protoplasm. The nucleus and the cytoplasm in the cells you have seen are parts of the protoplasm. Have you formed any impression of what protoplasm is like, from your work with cells? Protoplasm is very largely water, but containing many other dissolved and suspended substances, some of them of very complicated kinds. If you are able to examine under the microscope a small piece of Canadian Pondweed leaf, where the cells are quite large and easy to see, you may be able to detect streaming of the cell contents around the inside of the wall. This is a sign of the slimy, semi-liquid nature of protoplasm, rather like a table jelly which has just failed to set. Very recent researches, using the tremendous magnifications of the electron microscope, have shown that the internal structure of protoplasm is enormously complex; many biologists are finding this area of study, in which rapid progress has been made in the last few years, very fascinating indeed.

Now we have come to the end of our survey of what it means to say 'alive'. As we study more biology, we shall learn more about these activities, and the way they are carried on in different forms of life. Our immediate task, however, is to look more closely at two examples of highly developed living organisms, a flowering plant and a mammal. We choose these for two reasons; the mammals and the flowering plants occupy the major places in the world of nature, and yet they represent two very different ways of life.

Four

One way of life

It is time for us to examine, not aspects of life, but an example of one particular and very widespread form of life. All around us, in woods, meadows, roadsides, lawns and flower borders, are the great variety of kinds, and vast numbers of individuals, of the flowering plants.

Before beginning anything else, put a few seeds, such as cress, to germinate in a covered dish containing wet blotting paper. Leave them in a warm room for 4–5 days. They will be required a little later on.

Now we want you to look at well-developed plants of a grass, a carrot, and an antirrhinum (for alternatives see foot-note). If you can, examine these as found growing. Take a firm hold of the above-ground parts, near to soil level, and give a steady pull. Does the plant just come away, or is there a resistance to your pull? When a cow is feeding it pulls at grasses, holding them between the teeth of its lower jaw and a hard pad in its upper jaw. Usually the grass stems break off; the whole plant is not pulled up. Strong winds, too, affect plants; we see them sway and bend before the wind but only rarely does one blow right over.

Dig up a specimen of antirrhinum now, and then carefully wash away the soil from around the roots. If, when you pulled on the plant, you had succeeded in uprooting it, a great many of the more slender roots would have broken off and remained clinging tightly to the particles of soil. Even now you will find that many small grains of soil are so firmly held that they are very hard to wash off without damaging the plant.

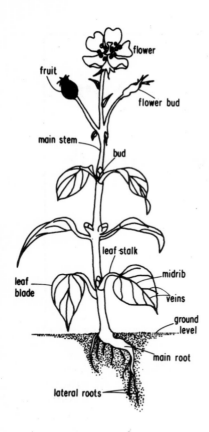

labels on figure:
flower
fruit
flower bud
main stem
bud
leaf stalk
midrib
leaf blade
veins
ground level
main root
lateral roots

Fig. 9 Diagram of a green plant

If you are pitching a tent, you would need to fix it safely and securely to the ground so that it wouldn't easily be dislodged or blown down. To do this one attaches the guy ropes to well driven-in pegs, spread out around the tent, to provide anchorage from all directions. Examine the root system of your plant. What is the position of the main root in the soil? What is the position and angle to the main root of the side or lateral roots? Illustrate the layout of the root system by making a drawing, adding the necessary explanatory labelling. (Fig. 9 is a diagram of a plant to show root and other features. It is not an antirrhinum or indeed any particular plant).

Lift the grass plant from the soil and examine its roots. What difference from antirrhinum can you see here? Is there a main root? Do the roots penetrate as deeply in the soil as those of antirrhinum?

Look at the carrot root system. What is its chief feature? How does this plant achieve anchorage in the soil?

This is the point at which you need to examine, with the aid of a hand lens, the germinated seeds in your dish. What can you see on the sides of the root which has emerged from the seed? You can expect to find a mass of fine white hairs – we call these root hairs – which are found only on young roots, a little way behind the growing tips. There can be as many as 300 to the square centimetre, and new ones are constantly growing out to replace the older ones which are dying off. Root hairs are so delicate, and so tightly woven around the fine grains of soil, that most of them are broken off when a plant is removed from the ground.

What is the function of root hairs? Their close contact with the soil is necessary because the soil is the source of the water and mineral salts which the plant needs. Root hairs absorb these substances, which are then transported through the roots to the above-ground parts. Some roots carry out another function. Think again of a carrot and the use we make of it. Do you know what that function is?

Stems

Above the ground is a stem, or sometimes a number of stems, which when young is green and comparatively soft, but which tends to become increasingly woody and tough with age. This is seen very clearly if one compares the plant which you are studying with say, a cress seedling and a tree. In your specimen, you should be able to detect a difference between the tips of the branches, the places where growth occurs, which are thin, soft and tender, and the lower parts, which are thicker and tougher.

If you can look at a balsam plant (the familiar house plant 'busy lizzie' is one of these), the stem of which is partly transparent, you should be able to see dark lines running up the stem. Do any enter the stalk of a leaf? Alternatively, take an outer stalk from a celery plant and break it in half. Usually this exposes 'strings' inside the stalk. The dark lines and the strings are both channels which bring a continual supply of water and salts from the roots to the aerial parts, and others which convey manufactured foodstuffs needed for energy production or growth to all parts of the plant, including the roots. They also help to support the stem because their walls are strengthened by woody material. Stems must be able to withstand the forces of wind and rain in order to hold up the leaves to the sunlight and to bear the flowers aloft where insects can see and visit them. The larger the bulk of the plant, the greater the weight to be supported, and so the stems must become thickened and strengthened by adding more woody materials inside. A larger number of conducting channels must be provided to satisfy the increased demand for water and foodstuffs.

Leaves

What features do the leaves of a grass, an antirrhinum, and a horse-chestnut have in common? Consider the colour, the amount of surface, and their thickness.

The colour of leaves is also that of the young stem and even the young flower buds, but contrasts with that of the root system. Without chlorophyll, to which the green colour of the plant is due, the plant would be unable to use energy from sunlight. This energy is used in producing sugars from carbon dioxide and water; the greatest amount of chlorophyll is present in the leaves, which are the principal site of food manufacture.

How does the shape of a leaf help in trapping light? Does the way the leaf is held on the plant help? Not only are leaves spread out but they are often so arranged that they shade one another as little as possible. This distribution of the leaves is sometimes so efficient that very little light passes through, as is shown by the deep shade under the trees in a beech wood, where very few small plants are able to survive.

Look now at the underside of one leaf. This surface shows most clearly the midrib and the smaller veins, which help to hold the leaf shape, and also connect with the transport channels of leaf stalk and stem. Make a careful drawing to show leaf shape, the leaf stalk, and the pattern of the veins.

Blow into the stalk of a buttercup leaf, the blade of which is held under water. Look for the appearance of air bubbles at places on the leaf surface. As an alternative, break off an onion leaf, which is hollow, push one end of a length of glass tubing into the central cavity and blow down the tube. The leaf contains many air spaces, which are in communication with the external air by many minute pores in the leaf's surface. When we blow into the leaf stalk the pressure forces air out through these pores, which are usually most numerous on the lower surface. Through the pores pass the gases needed or given off in photosynthesis and respiration and so does the water vapour lost by evaporation.

Flowers

The flowers, which later give rise to the fruits and seeds, are the means whereby a new generation of plants is produced, to carry on the life of that type, and also to spread it to new areas. The reproduction of flowering plants we shall consider in more detail in a later chapter.

Five

Another way of life

We have taken a look at the general structure of a flowering plant and now we turn our attention to an animal. Amongst the great variety of animals, there are many different patterns of structure. Some have a skeleton, others do not. The general structure of a worm, for instance, differs greatly from that of a snail and that again from a bee. In turn these differ from those animals which have their skeleton inside – the bony animals. Even here there are several different groups. However, the group which probably interests us most, because we ourselves belong to it, as do most of our domesticated animals, is that of the mammals. We shall therefore begin by considering the appearance and way of life of one of the mammals. In the description here the dog is used, but what is said will be generally correct for any other mammal you may find it more convenient to examine – cat, guinea pig, rabbit, and so on. What is certain is that we must have a live example to study!

Look at your specimen. We all know it is an animal, but consider what features enable us to say at once that it is an animal. For one thing, it hasn't got the shape and parts typical of a plant! You may well be able to suggest some other reasons straightaway; perhaps more answers will be clear by the end of the chapter.

Has your animal been content to stay motionless? I would be rather surprised if it had, for most mammals give one an impression of alertness, and of active movement. What else can we discover by looking at the outside of our specimen?

Into what main regions is the whole body divided?

Inside the body there are many organs such as the brain, the heart, the lungs, the stomach, and so on; as we cannot observe these from the outside, their position is shown in Fig. 10. The existence of four limbs will be obvious enough, but there are several other points to look for here. Humans have the whole of the foot, from toe to heel, resting upon the ground, but some mammals only put the toes on the ground.

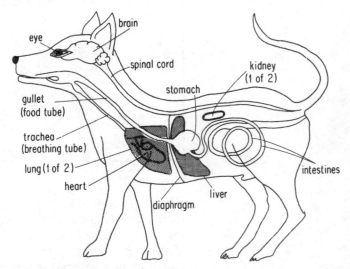

Fig. 10   The mammal and its organs, drawn from the left-hand side. No part of the skeleton is shown

Furthermore there are others, such as the horse, in which only the thick and toughened toe nail, the hoof, is in contact with the ground. Which of these possibilities applies in the case of your specimen? Has it flat nails, claws, or hooves?

What joints can you recognise on the fore and the hind limb? Compare the limbs with your own to identify the elbow, knee, and other joints.

Look at the underside of the foot. What is the skin like there? What value is this to the animal?

Mammals are active creatures, and active animals require lots of quickly-provided information about what's going on around them. This is supplied by the sense organs. What sense organs can you find on the animal? What sorts of information does the mammal obtain from them?

You will have noticed that the mammal is covered, apart from a few special places (where are they?), with hair, often of characteristic colour. In many mammals there are long guard hairs and more numerous but shorter body hairs. Can you find these types?

Hold the specimen for a little while; decide from this whether it has the same body temperature as the outside, is colder or warmer than the outside air.

Biologists describe mammals as 'warm-blooded'; by this we mean that they maintain a constant internal temperature whether the external temperature rises or falls. A 'cold-blooded' animal, such as a frog, has a body temperature which varies with that of the surroundings; it cannot cool off when too hot, and in cold weather becomes inactive. Mammals can regulate their temperature by methods of heat loss (such as sweating), or conserving heat (such as the insulating effect of hair). Some mammals have very little hair, the work of insulation being taken over by layers of fat below the skin (the blubber of whales is an example), but we ourselves use clothing to supply the deficiency.

Another thing one can observe is the quickly-repeated rise and fall of the front part of the body, the chest region. No doubt you know that these are the breathing movements whereby the animal takes air into its body for its respiration. The breathing movements are helped by an elastic partition which stretches across the middle of the trunk. This is known as the diaphragm, and it separates the chest or thorax with the lungs and heart from the abdomen containing the other organs.

When we come to examine the internal structure of the dog we find that, in common with fish, amphibians, reptiles, birds, as well as other mammals, the body is supported by a skeleton made up of a large number of separate bones. Some of these bones are fairly near the surface, and you can feel them beneath the skin in the limbs. Find at least five places where your own bones can be felt.

The skeleton holds up the body, and by means of the pull of muscles attached to the bones, the dog operates a kind of lever system when it wishes to move. The skeleton also helps to protect parts of the body, as in the skull which contains the delicate and vital sustance of the brain.

One of the main parts of the skeleton is the backbone – not a single bone, but a chain of interlocked bones, the vertebrae, in a row from immediately behind the head to the far tip of the tail. These vertebrae are not all exactly alike in shape, but are modified for various tasks; for instance, the first two are so shaped that they enable the head to move up and down and from side to side. Examine an assembled mammal skeleton, and find the parts mentioned. Make a diagram, using simplified shapes to show the main parts of the skeleton – skull, backbone, front and rear limbs. Note, too, how the bones move on one another by means of the joints. Try moving your own limbs and feel the muscles doing the work; for example, raise your right forearm while holding the upper arm at a point about six inches below the shoulder with your left hand. You can feel the muscle there swelling as it contracts to pull up the forearm.

In an earlier chapter we said that the power to reproduce is a universal attribute of living things. In the mammals the eggs develop inside the body of the mother and the young are born alive at a more or less advanced state of development.

The puppy is able to stand and move about within a few hours of its birth, but the human infant is not able to walk until a year or more after birth. Whether helpless or active when born, the young are fed at first on a special fluid, milk, produced by the mother in her mammary glands. Milk provides the young with all kinds of food material they need; it is a 'complete food.'

As the puppy grows, teeth push upwards in its jaws and it becomes able to tackle a solid diet; no doubt among the wild ancestors of our domestic dogs this would at first be the already killed carcases of the prey caught by the mother. As the puppy became stronger it would take part in the hunting, until fully able to fend for itself. Having caught its food, with the aid of the long, pointed canine teeth, the meat is cut into lumps by the back teeth, but is not chewed. A dog 'bolts' its food, a relic of behaviour from its ancestry, where the pack gathered at a kill, and each one struggled for as large a share as possible. The food is broken down into usable components in a long coiled tube, the alimentary canal; insoluble wastes are passed out as dung, and dissolved wastes are excreted in the fluid urine.

We have now mentioned all the characteristics of living matter in relation to two highly organised, very complex examples, a mammal and a flowering plant; in spite of the great apparent differences in form, the same living processes occur in each case.

To finish this section, let us check on the major differences between an 'animal' and a 'plant'. In so doing, we ought to remember that whatever points we suggest, there are likely to be some apparent exceptions, which can only be understood from a wide knowledge of biology. Further, there exist microscopic creatures which are in some ways plant-like and in other ways animal-like. The distinction between the two kinds is not as hard-and-fast as we might suppose.

In the table, on the next page some blanks have been left quite intentionally. From what you have learned, you should be able to say what should fill the blanks (but if you write down the missing words do so on a piece of paper, not in the book).

Differences between Plants and Animals

Animals have the power of locomotion; they can move towards something favourable or away from something which is unfavourable.

Plants remain in the same place; they can only ..... towards or away from external influence.

Animals cannot manufacture their food requirements from simple materials. They must obtain complex foodstuffs by eating other animals or plants.

Plants can manufacture all their food from simple materials present in soil and..... using ..... from sunlight to do so.

Because they need to move around freely, animal bodies are of a ..... shape.

The bodies of plants are spread out to give a very large area for absorbing light and gases from the air, together with ..... and ..... from the soil.

Growth occurs all over the animal's body.

Growth only occurs in limited areas, just..... the tips of roots and shoots.

Six

Nutrition and Respiration

Experiment 9. Does our breath contain carbon dioxide?

Take some clear limewater in a beaker and allow some carbon dioxide gas, produced by the action of dilute hydrochloric acid on chalk, to bubble into it (see Fig. 11). Note carefully how the limewater changes in appearance. Limewater is used to detect the presence of carbon dioxide in this way.

Using some fresh limewater, blow into it several times through a glass tube. Do you get the same result?

If carbon dioxide can be shown to be present in the air we breathe out of our bodies, how can we be sure that it was not present in the same amount in the air we had breathed in? Take the simple piece of apparatus shown in Fig. 12, and breathe in and out *gently* several times. As you will see, the apparatus is so designed that air is drawn in through one flask, but is blown out through the other one. Use clear limewater in both flasks. After breathing in and out a number of times, compare the limewater in the two flasks. Does milkiness appear in both, in only one, or even in none? Do you consider the results show that we release carbon dioxide in the breath we give out?

Experiment 10. Do other kinds of living things give off carbon dioxide?

Here is a way of finding out. Place about an inch of clear limewater in the bottom of a gas jar, and suspend in the jar a dampened muslin bag containing several live earthworms (see Fig. 13). Close the jar by means of a greased gas jar lid, which will give an airtight seal. Leave for an hour or two. Does the limewater turn milky? How would you set up a control experiment to show that the result was due to the presence of the worms, and not to the air in the jar? Try this experiment again with plant material – soaked pea seeds are very suitable, but a longer time will be needed than for the animals.

How, and from what is this carbon dioxide produced? To make carbon dioxide requires a source of carbon, and one of oxygen. For instance when coal, which is very largely carbon, is burned in air, which contains oxygen, carbon dioxide is produced. Where do the carbon and the oxygen for the carbon dioxide produced by living things come from? To begin with, do living things use the oxygen from the air?

Experiment 11. To find if exhaled breath is poor in oxygen.

Invert a large gas jar of air in a trough of water and use

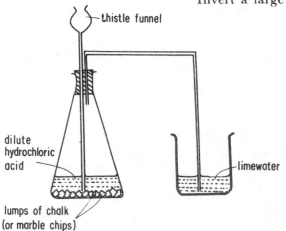

Fig. 11 Apparatus to supply carbon dioxide

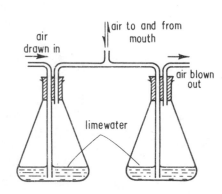

Fig. 12 Apparatus for testing breath for carbon dioxide

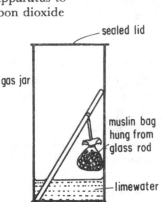

Fig. 13 Apparatus to find if small living organisms release carbon dioxide

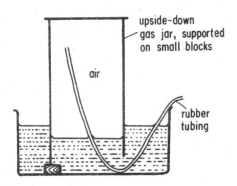

Fig. 14 Apparatus to find if breath is poor in oxygen

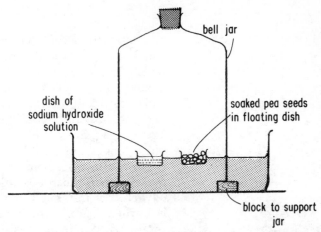

Fig. 15 Apparatus to find if seeds use oxygen. The control apparatus is not shown. The small blocks allow free circulation of water between the trough and the bell jar

a length of clean rubber tubing to draw into your lungs the air from this jar (see Fig. 14). Breathe the air out again through the same tube into the jar, and repeat the process several times. Remove the tube, place a lid on the gas jar, and turn it the right way up. Hold in it a lighted wood splint. What happens? Compare the result with a burning splint placed in a jar of unaltered air. A lighted splint requires oxygen to keep it burning. What, then, do you conclude about the air you breathe out?

Experiment 12. To find if soaked seeds use up oxygen.

Soak some pea seeds for 1–2 days and then place them in the apparatus as shown in Fig. 15. Sodium hydroxide solution is present because this absorbs any carbon dioxide given off. This is necessary so that we can see any change in air volume caused by the using-up of oxygen. We shall not *see* any change in the sodium hydroxide, but we use it in preference to lime-water because it can absorb more carbon dioxide than an equal volume of limewater.

Leave the apparatus for 2 days. Is there a rise in the water level in the tube? Does any such rise match the known pro-portion of oxygen in air (one-fifth)? See if a lighted splint will continue to burn, or go out, when placed in the end of the tube. Use a second or control apparatus, set up in exactly the same way except for the seeds, to check your results.

If we have shown that living things release carbon dioxide, and that they use oxygen, we must ask why they do so, and where the carbon comes from. The function of respiration is to release energy, energy which the organisms can use to 'drive' their other body activities. Oxygen is used to break up foodstuffs, these all being compounds of carbon, and some of this carbon is turned into carbon dioxide.

Because of their active movement, animals require much larger amounts of energy than plants, and so carry on much more rapid respiration. To obtain enough oxygen for this we, and very many other animals, make breathing movements to increase the rate at which oxygen enters and carbon dioxide leaves the body. What happens to your breathing rate when you go on a run, or play in a fast game? Can you account for this?

We have said that respiration requires foodstuffs, but where do living things get these? The short answer is that plants make them, but animals eat them.

In an earlier chapter we said that the principal region of food manufacture in a plant is the leaves, and that carbon dioxide from the air, light, and water and mineral salts from the soil are necessary for this to occur. We should not be content simply to accept statements like these, but should seek to prove their correctness by suitable tests.

The first step here is to find some means of showing whether or not food has been made in the leaf. Many, although not all, leaves accumulate grains of starch during the hours of daylight; these grains can be observed in the cells of plants, e.g. in a potato, when very thin slices (what the biologist calls 'sections') are cut and examined under the microscope (see Fig. 16). Fortunately, starch is a substance which can be easily identified.

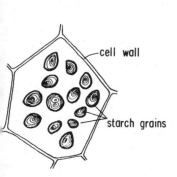

16 Starch grains in a potato Note how the grains consist of layer upon layer of starch

Experiment 13. To show the test for starch.

Take a sample of starch powder on a white tile, or some other light-coloured background, and add to it iodine solution. The white starch now becomes an intense purplish-black. Repeat the test using some other substances, such as sugar or milk powder: do you get this dark colour? Having shown that the iodine test identifies starch, we can now use it to find out whether starch is present in a leaf, freshly picked from a plant.

Experiment 14. To test a leaf for the presence of starch.

Detach a leaf from a geranium, or other plant with softish leaves, which has been growing in normal conditions and has been in daylight for some hours. Lay the leaf on a tile and pour on iodine solution; then let it run off; no definite result can be seen, because the solution has not been able to penetrate the leaf. It is, in fact, necessary to carry out two preliminary operations. First, to kill the leaf cells so that fluids can get in; second, to remove the green pigment, chlorophyll, so that the test result can easily be seen.

Take another leaf and, holding it with forceps, dip it into

boiling water for about half a minute or until it becomes limp. This will kill the leaf cells and enable fluids to enter easily.

Next the leaf must be boiled in white methylated spirits (nearly pure alcohol) until all the chlorophyll has been extracted, which may take 5 minutes or so. Methylated spirits very easily catches fire, and *must not* be heated directly over a Bunsen flame. The tube containing it and the leaf should be suspended in a bath of boiling water, preferably heated by electricity, such as a hotplate, or an immersion heater.

When the leaf comes out of the alcohol it will be hard and brittle so your next step is to wash it well in water, before spreading it flat on a tile.

Now pour on the iodine solution. If you have carried out each step correctly, the blue-black colour can be expected to appear. What is your conclusion for this experiment?

Experiment 15. What happens to the starch in a darkened plant?

What would happen if the plant whose leaves we have been testing were deprived of light? Put the plant in a dark cupboard for 48 hours, and then test another leaf in exactly the same way as before. Is there still any starch present? What does this suggest?

If the plant is kept in the dark for longer times, even though it is watered well, it soon looks very unhealthy, the leaves begin to turn yellow, and the plant declines until it dies. It will, in fact, have become starved, because it has been prevented from making any more food.

Experiment 16. To show that the plant must have carbon dioxide in order to manufacture its food.

Using the information gained from the last experiment, we make a geranium plant use up all its stores of starch by keeping it in the dark for 48 hours. The idea is to put the plant in an atmosphere which has no carbon dioxide, and see if it can now make starch.

A fairly simple way of doing this is shown in Fig. 17. The sodium hydroxide solution takes up all the carbon dioxide from the air under the bell jar, and sealing the jar with a grease on to a glass plate prevents the entry of any more. It is necessary to have a second plant, also destarched, under another bell jar, but without the sodium hydroxide solution, to show that a plant can make starch while under such a jar. It is important that this second version, known as the *control experiment*, differs in only one thing from the first version. In this way we can check that the result we obtain is produced by the factor we are investigating, and not by some other circumstance which is unsuspected or overlooked.

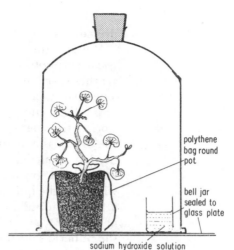

polythene
bag round
pot

bell jar
sealed to
glass plate

sodium hydroxide solution

Fig. 17 Apparatus to deprive a plant of carbon dioxide. The bag, which is tied round the stem of the plant, prevents the escape of carbon dioxide from the soil

Leave both of your jars in good light for 2–3 hours, then test a leaf from each for the presence of starch. Have you shown that carbon dioxide is essential for starch formation?

The proportion of carbon dioxide in air is very small (only 3 parts in 10,000) but green plants are able to combine it with water to form foodstuffs. At the same time they release oxygen. If you look at underwater plants on a bright day, you can see the many small bubbles of oxygen rising from them.

A plant in light, then, makes starch. But is this always true? Repeat the starch test on an onion leaf from a plant growing under normal conditions. Can we say now that all green plants make starch? If some plants do not produce starch, what substances do they make in light? Scientists have shown that starch can be split up by chemical methods into a soluble substance known as a simple sugar. Do green plants make sugars in light, and some of them turn the sugar into insoluble starch for storage? Let us see if any simple sugar is present in a second leaf from the onion.

Experiment 17. To test for a simple sugar in an onion leaf which has been in light.

Chop up the leaf and crush the pieces with about 2 inches in a test tube of distilled water. Filter off the solid matter and to the liquid obtained add Fehling's solution. To prevent it spoiling before use, this is kept in two separate parts. Add about ¼″ of each, shake gently to mix well, and heat the mixture carefully until it boils. Fehling's solution can burn your fingers; if any does get on your hands, wash it off at once with running water; use a test-tube holder when heating. If a rusty-brown sediment forms in the tube, simple sugars were

35

present. Is it possible that plants manufacture sugar in light?

We call the process of food manufacture by leaves, *photo-synthesis* (photo—from the Greek word *photos*, meaning light: synthesis—from the Greek words *syn*, with, and *thesis*, putting). The term therefore indicates a building-up process which requires light energy. We can regard photosynthesis as a way of storing the energy of light, energy which can be released for use when the plant respires some of its sugars. When not needed immediately, sugar is often turned to starch which forms solid grains, convenient for storage. From the sugar, which can be quickly obtained back from starch when needed, a plant can build all the other complicated chemicals it must have. For many of these manufactures it also needs some of the mineral salts taken in by the roots.

Unlike a plant, the animal has no powers of using simple raw materials to make its food supply; it needs a ready-made food source. A lion gets it in the form of fresh meat, a cow as grass, you and I as the variety of foods in our daily meals. In none of these cases can use be made of the food until it has been broken down into simple substances, in the digestive system. The digestive system produces various fluids, such as the gastric juices made by the stomach, to help in the breakdown of food. Then the blood carries the useful material from the food to every part of the body.

It isn't satisfactory, however, for us just to eat until our stomachs are full; we need a 'complete diet'. That is, sufficient of each of several different kinds of food requirement. Here is the list:

Carbohydrates	Used to provide energy through respiration (refer back to p. 12).
Fats	Help to insulate the body and so keep us warm. They can also be used to provide energy.
Proteins	Needed for making new cells, and therefore for growth, as well as for replacing worn out or damaged cells.
Mineral salts	Needed in smaller amounts for various purposes, such as calcium phosphate for bones.
Vitamins	The body requires only minute amounts of these, but they are vital for healthy life.

In addition to the above, the body needs water, which is the major part, by weight, of protoplasm, and is also used to carry dissolved substances around the body. The digestive system must have some bulky material, which we term roughage, to keep its muscles working properly in moving food along. We shall not be able to feed on small pills alone, however rich their contents!

Some kinds of food contain much of one requirement, less or none of another; by eating a varied diet we can ensure that we get enough of each kind. A good supply of fresh foods is very desirable since some vitamins are quite quickly destroyed as food becomes stale, or when it is cooked.

While the detection of mineral substances and vitamins in foods is often a rather complicated business, we can quite easily carry out tests for the presence of proteins, carbohydrates or fats.

Experiment 18. To test for protein in foods.

When a foodstuff containing protein is heated with the colourless solution known as Millon's reagent, a dark red solid forms at the bottom of the tube, or on the sides of the food itself. Try this test with, say, egg white, lean meat, or milk. Use a very small piece of the food – pea size – or a few drops of liquid, with $\frac{1}{2}''$ of the reagent in a test-tube. Heat the tube carefully over a Bunsen flame, shaking the tube gently to keep the contents mixed and so preventing them from spurting out. Millon's reagent is poisonous; keep it off yourself and your books; if any should be spilled on the bench, mop it up straightaway with a wet cloth; wash your hands well when you finish your practical work.

This is how to write up your work:

Test	Observations	Conclusions
A little egg white was heated with Millon's reagent	A dark red sediment (precipitate) formed on heating	Protein is present in egg white

If a test gives a negative result, do NOT write down 'nothing happened'; state what you did see, and then give the appropriate conclusion, e.g. 'protein was absent.'

Experiment 19. To test for carbohydrates.

Starch and sugars are carbohydrates, but they require different test methods. You have already used the iodine test for starch in a leaf. To use it on foodstuffs, it is quite sufficient to add the iodine solution to the food material, without previous treatments. Try it on a slice cut from a potato.

Similarly, you have already tried the Fehling's test for simple sugars. Try it now with milk, or with a small piece of carrot. Domestic sugar, however, is not a simple sugar and foods in which it has been used for sweetening do not give a positive result to this test. Try the test with granulated sugar, and see for yourself. Now take a second sample of the sugar, dissolve it in distilled water, add about 3 drops of dilute hydrochloric acid, and boil for a few seconds. Allow the mixture to cool, add three drops of dilute sodium hydroxide solution to remove the acid, and then carry out the Fehling's test as before. Do you now obtain a positive result? The boiling with acid splits the domestic sugar into simple sugars. There would be no point in doing this if we had already found simple sugars to be present.

Experiment 20. To test for fats.

The presence of fats may be shown by squashing a little of the food on to a piece of filter paper. This leaves a mark which if it is watery will dry away, but if it is fatty will remain and be somewhat translucent (lets light through). Remember the marks that fish and chips leave on newspaper?

Material to be tested for fat can be crushed and shaken in a test tube with one inch of benzene, which dissolves fat, and a spot of the benzene then dropped on a piece of filter paper. Make a second spot with pure benzene and allow both spots to dry. Compare them; if they are alike the test is negative. If the first spot leaves a shiny greasy mark, the test is positive and fat was present. Try this test with crushed peanuts or sunflower seeds.

If you have the time, you can test parts of your diet to determine the presence or absence of proteins, carbohydrates or fats. Record the tests and results in the manner shown.

Lastly, a small experiment to show the effect of one of the digestive juices of the body.

Experiment 21. To study the effect of saliva on starch.

Take a very small amount of 1% starch solution. Add one drop of iodine solution on a tile, to show that your starch solution does give the blue-black colour. To the remainder, say 4 or 5 drops of it, add some distilled water which you have rinsed around your mouth to obtain some saliva. At ten minute intervals add a drop of this mixture to another drop of iodine solution on the tile. Does it still give the black colour? If so, wait another 10 minutes and then try again. If the starch-iodine colour no longer appears, then you will know that the starch has all been broken down by a digestive agent present in the saliva. Has the starch been split up into sugars? Try the Fehling's test on the remainder of the mixture.

Saliva is only one of a number of digestive juices which our body produces; all animals which eat complicated foodstuffs need such juices in order to reduce their food to simple units which their bodies can use.

Seven

Setting up an aquarium

Most of us get a good deal of interest and indeed pleasure out of watching the living inhabitants of an aquarium. To set up a thriving aquarium is not difficult, provided we bear in mind some of the things we have already learned about biology. In the account which follows, it is assumed that we shall be using living things collected from local ponds, lakes or streams, as was done in setting up the aquarium shown in Fig. 18. If your personal taste is towards something more exotic, such as warm water tanks for tropical fish, or marine aquaria, then you will need to consult other sources of information. Your local library is a good place to start.

To establish a healthy aquarium life we must use the knowledge we have gained in our studies. For instance, at least some of the plants in our aquarium will need anchorage for their roots. They will all need light, carbon dioxide and mineral salts in order to make their food and to grow. They will give off oxygen during photosynthesis.

The animals will require a supply of food. Some of them can obtain it by nibbling at the plants; others will eat pieces of debris and decaying material – these we call the 'scavengers'. Some animals eat other animals, but we shall think twice about introducing these types to our tanks. Animals will also need oxygen for their respiration, but will give off carbon dioxide. Their waste products will provide a supply of mineral salts for the plants.

Steps to take:

1. Begin by thoroughly cleaning a glass tank, using soapy

warm water and a stiff brush, followed by thorough rinsing with clean water. This will remove all dirt, grease, and anything likely to be harmful to life.

2. Most aquatic plants, like those on land, need anchorage. True, there are a few plants which will live happily unattached, as they do in nature, such as Canadian pond weed. For the others we should provide some solid base material into which the roots can penetrate. Soil, especially that containing clayey material, is unsatisfactory because fine particles from it cause cloudiness in the water, which can last almost indefinitely, and re-occur whenever the soil is disturbed. It is better to use sand or small gravel which you have washed well to remove sediments.

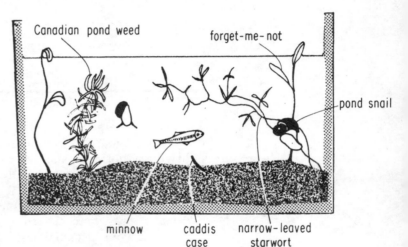

Fig. 18 Aquarium tank set up by two students in the manner described in the text, using material from local sources

3. The water can be added now. If you can use pond water, or clean rain water, this is excellent. In many areas, tap water contains dissolved calcium bicarbonate which in time will leave a white deposit of chalk on the side of the aquarium. It can be used, but should be allowed to stand for a couple of days; during this time the tap water will lose its chlorine content. To avoid disturbing the sand or gravel, pour the water on to a sheet of paper.

4. So far we have provided water and anchorage for plants; carbon dioxide will also be available, dissolved in the water. The aquarium must be placed in a part of the room which receives moderate light. If some direct sunlight falls on the tank this will help the plants, but too much strong sun is not desirable, as it can damage them.

5. What plants shall we use? Canadian pondweed is a good oxygenator, which remains submerged; so does water moss (*Fontinalis*). Duckweed floats on the top, and is useful in small amounts but if it is allowed to multiply too freely it will cover the whole surface. Useful plants whose roots must be spread out in the gravel include curled pondweed and water starwort (see Fig. 19). After planting allow the aquarium to stand for a few days before adding any animals.

6. What animals can we put in? Our work on nutrition and respiration tells us that two important factors must be kept in

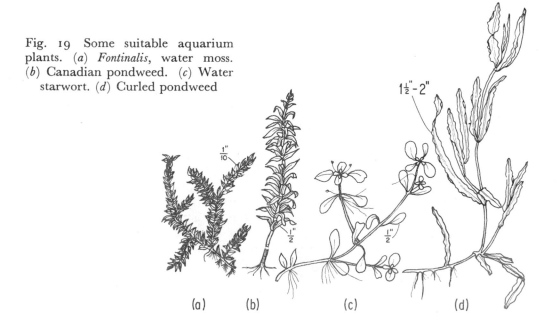

Fig. 19 Some suitable aquarium plants. (*a*) *Fontinalis*, water moss. (*b*) Canadian pondweed. (*c*) Water starwort. (*d*) Curled pondweed

(a)   (b)   (c)   (d)

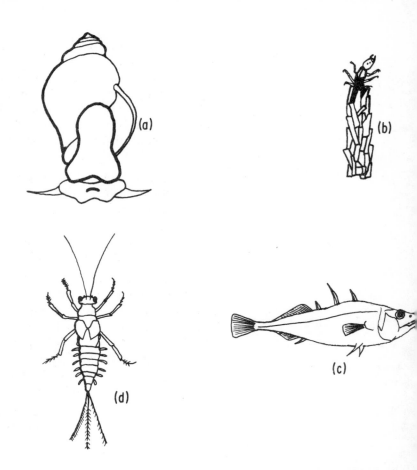

Fig. 20 Some freshwater animals. (*a*) Pond snail. (*b*) Caddis larva
in case of debris. (*c*) Stickleback. (*d*) Mayfly larva

mind – food and oxygen. If our animals are vegetarians, they
must not be so large or so numerous that their consumption
exceeds the plants' capacity for growth. We must also be careful over the choice of flesh-eaters, or we shall find the animals'
stocks rapidly dwindling.

Again, the animals must not be so numerous or so active
that they require more oxygen than is present in the water
available. We can, of course, increase the supply of oxygen
by using an air pump (excellent electrically operated aerators
can be obtained at moderate prices), and we shall need to do
so if we want to keep very active animals. A good general-
isation to keep in mind is that creatures whose native home is
quick-running water will require much more oxygen than
those from sluggish or still waters.

Pond snails, which exist in various types, are valuable because they will scrape off the minute green plants which tend
to accumulate on the glass sides of the aquarium. Caddis-fly
larvae, with their do-it-yourself cases of debris or sand grains,

are interesting; most of them feed on small pieces of plant material. Mayfly larvae move quite actively around the bottom, and many of them have 'gills' projecting down both sides of the body; the food is chiefly vegetable matter, although some may eat dead animals.

Fish? They add great interest but we must be careful not to overstock. 24 square inches of water surface per 1 inch of fish length is a safe rule. The stickleback is probably easier to keep than the minnow, but both are flesh-feeders, small aquatic insects and crustaceans making up the bulk of their normal diet. As the aquarium itself will hardly contain enough supplies, we shall have to add water fleas, very small worms, or tiny pieces of raw meat, but don't put in more than they can consume. Uneaten flesh rots and fouls the water.

Some animals whose introduction is likely to cause trouble include leeches, dragonfly larvae and water boatmen. Leeches attach themselves to the bodies of other animals, pierce the skin and suck blood. Dragonfly larvae and water boatmen are very destructive flesh eaters, which catch and kill other pond animals.

This list of plants and animals (some of the latter are illustrated in Fig. 20) is by no means exhaustive. You can find out more by consulting reference books such as Clegg's *The Freshwater Life of the British Isles*, published by Warne, and of course by your own investigations.

7. Keeping it going. We are aiming for a balance between the numbers and output of the plants and those of the animals. It will be necessary to add to, or to take away from, the populations in order to achieve this. Particularly, if the water starts to become cloudy and foul, cut down the numbers of plants and animals. If it seems necessary to change the water, this is best done by syphoning, holding the aquarium end of the syphon close to, but not in contact with, the sand or gravel.

When you have got the aquarium going well, you will in fact have made a living model of the larger world, with its 'balance of nature', in which the relationships of animals and plants are tightly interwoven. As time goes on, your observations of the aquarium will enable you to work out a 'what feeds on what' plan for its inhabitants.

Eight

From flower to seed

Many insects, large and small, are dependent on flowers for their food supply, visiting them for the sweet, sugary fluid known as nectar, or the flower's pollen. The hive bee, for instance sucks the nectar up a long tongue into its mouth, and swallows it. In a special stomach the nectar is partially digested to form the honey which will then be stored in the honeycombs of the hive. The bee also collects much of the pollen which has fallen on to its body and legs, and uses this to form 'bee-bread', a food for adult and young bees. Some of the pollen, however, escapes this fate and may be transferred to another flower, an essential step in the plant's reproduction. The structure of a flower is, in fact, adapted to ensuring that a transfer of pollen does occur, and this is what we shall be investigating.

Let us begin with the buttercup, a plant with which many of us are no doubt familiar. Collect a few good specimens of the flower, and take them apart stage by stage, beginning at the bottom, where the outmost parts are attached to the swollen end of the flower-stalk, the receptacle.

First of all, we find the ring of sepals. How many? What is their colour? Are they separate, or joined to one another? Write your findings in a table with four columns, like this:

Part of flower	Number	Brief Description	Function
Sepals	5	Green, rather leaf-like, pointed	Protect bud

44

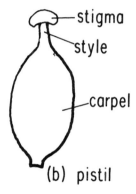

(a) stamen

(b) pistil

Fig. 21   Reproductive
parts of a flower

The function of the sepals is the protection of the other floral structures while the flower is in the bud stage.

The next structures are the petals. Examine these and record the same items of information as for the sepals. We can think of the brightly coloured, conspicuous petals as providing a clear 'signal' for passing insects that here is a source of food, the sugary solution called nectar. In the buttercup the nectar is produced in a flap-like nectary at the base of each petal. This patch can be seen to have a glistening appearance in a fresh-picked flower.

Thirdly, we come to the stamens. Each can be seen to have a head, the anther, on top of the stalk, the filament. When ripe the anthers split open, releasing a yellow dust called the pollen. If an insect visits the flower, some of this dust gets caught on its body and may later be transferred to other flowers of the same kind. Very large numbers of pollen grains are produced, because many never arrive at their destination, a stigma.

A stigma is the uppermost part of the pistil, at the centre of the flower. It is connected to the carpel by the style (see Fig. 21). Inside the carpel there is, in buttercups, a single ovule, which is capable of growing into a seed. This will only happen if insects visit the flowers, and in their wanderings in search of nectar, transfer pollen to the stigma.

A good way of describing the structure of a flower is by means of a simplified 'half-flower' drawing. To make one of these we cut a flower as nearly as possible into two equal halves. Looking at the cut surface, we attempt to draw what we see, the correct shapes of parts, and their position relative to one another. An example of this is given, with explanatory notes, in Fig. 22. It is *not* a buttercup, although our specimen is of generally similar construction, because I want you to work it out, and not just tamely copy from the book. Maybe in the past biology students have been required to do too

Fig. 22   Structure of a half-flower. It has 5 sepals and 5 petals in all, so there are $2\frac{1}{2}$ of each in a half-flower. Note that the attachment of sepals and petals alternates, so the half sepal appears at the opposite edge to the half petal

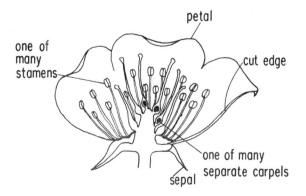

much drawing of specimens, until it has become a bit of a bore to them. Nevertheless, it still is an important and necessary way of recording vital information, so try and make a thorough job of it!

The buttercup is of rather small size, and although the open, cup shape makes the nectar easy to get, there is not much of it. Consequently, it is not often visited by bees. What insects do settle on it? Find out for yourself by observing plants growing in their native state. I suspect you will find that many of the visitors are small insects rather than the larger strong-flying ones.

Before we consider what happens after pollen has been transferred to a flower's stigma, we will examine a second flower, of a larger size and more complicated instruction. The *antirrhinum* or snapdragon is so arranged that it is likely to be successfully visited only by those large insects which are capable of strong flight, and therefore may distribute pollen further afield. The first thing to notice is the way the petals are joined into a tube with a kind of trapdoor mechanism. Watch where arriving insects (of what kind or kinds are they?) land on the flower, and how they manage to make an entry. When an insect leaves the petal tube, does the trapdoor close again? If so, how? Try to see what parts of the visitor have become dusted with pollen. Then open a flower, and try to spot the link between the position of the anthers and the pollen-dusted patches on the animal. Is the stigma in such a position as to brush off some of this pollen?

Also try to locate the nectary; note that there are large numbers of ovules inside the one compound ovary, which is made up of two joined-together carpels. Fig. 23 gives an outline of the halved petal tube with trapdoor, and the position of the sepals and the bases of the stamens. Trace or copy this figure and complete it by drawing in the rest of the stamens, the ovary, style, stigma, and nectary. Accompany your drawing by a short account explaining how the flower attracts its visitors and what happens on their arrival.

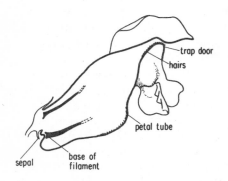

Fig. 23   Incomplete drawing of antirrhinum flower

Pollination and Fertilisation

The transfer of pollen from an anther to a stigma is termed *pollination*. In many plants it is achieved by the aid of insects, but in others the pollen is wind-borne; the grasses use this method, with unpleasant results for the unfortunate sufferer from hay-fever. Many plants have devices which favour cross-pollination, where the pollen comes from a different plant, as against self-pollination, using pollen from the same plant. In general, cross-pollination leads to more varied and often more vigorously-growing offspring than does self-pollination.

Once pollen has arrived on the stigma, a series of rather complicated events takes place, resulting in *fertilisation*. First a slender tube grows out of the pollen grain, and down the style towards the ovary.

Experiment 22. To observe the growth of pollen tubes.

Place a drop of 3% cane sugar solution (3g of household sugar dissolved in distilled water and made up to 100 ml of solution) in the centre of a cover glass and dust pollen grains from antirrhinum anthers onto it with the aid of a small brush. Turn the glass over carefully, and place it so that the drop is hanging into the hollow made by placing a ring of plasticine on a microscope slide (see Fig. 24). To prevent drying up of the drop, smear a little grease around the edges of the cover glass to seal it to the ring on the slide. Leave for several hours, or overnight. Examine the slide under a junior microscope. If all has gone well, you can expect to see long thread-like outgrowths from some of the pollen grains. The sugar acts as food for this growth, food which is normally provided by the stigma.

As the pollen tube grows down into the ovary, it carries inside it a small rounded body, the male nucleus. When the tip of the pollen tube reaches one ovule (see Fig. 25), it enters through the opening, the micropyle, and grows into the egg cell. Here the tip bursts, the male nucleus floats out, and soon fuses (merges) with the female nucleus of the egg-cell. This *joining of a male nucleus with a female nucleus* is *fertilisation*; it is a characteristic of sexual reproduction.

By the way, I found out that 3% cane sugar solution was suitable for growing antirrhinum pollen tubes by trying various strengths of sugar solution and watching them for tube growth. You could try this with other kinds of flower pollen. Make up 100 ml of 5% sugar solution, in the way described above, put aside 20 ml, and then prepare weaker solutions by adding water as shown in Table 2.

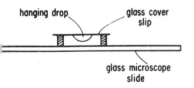

Fig. 24   Hanging drop culture

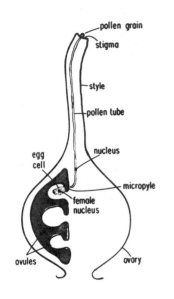

Fig. 25   Diagram of pollen tube growth

Table 2.   Volumes needed to make sugar solutions for pollen tube growth

Strength required	Volume of 5% sugar solution	Volume of distilled water
4%	20 ml	5 ml
3%	20 ml	13 ml
2%	20 ml	30 ml
1%	20 ml	80 ml

Then follow the procedure given for the antirrhinum pollen, putting each strength of solution in a separate dish.

47

Subsequent Development

Each of the ovules which has been fertilised (one pollen grain can fertilise only one ovule) is now capable of developing into a seed. Any ovules which have not been fertilised will not develop further and will soon shrivel. The combined nucleus formed by the act of fertilisation divides, as does the egg cell, many times. As a result the structures found in a seed, the plumule, radicle, and cotyledons, are formed, with much enlarging of the ovule. When the seed has become full-grown, the coat of the ovule becomes dry and hard, forming the seed-coat or testa.

Look at the flower after fertilisation has occurred – one sign that has taken place is the withering of the petals. Note down as many changes in the flower as you can find. What parts have withered; which fell off? Which remain and grow?

Did you observe the enlarged ovary? Cut one open – inside are the ripening seeds, enclosed in the changing ovary wall. In the antirrhinum, the enlarged ovary wall soon begins to dry out and become hard; similar development occurs in the buttercup. The whole structure is now called a fruit. Do you envisage a fruit as something brightly-coloured, juicy, and enjoyable to eat? Something like a plum or a grape? These contain seeds, but so do the dry, unpalatable seed-containing structures of an antirrhinum or a poppy, so we call them fruits too.

What is the purpose of a fruit? It is developed to assist in the spreading of the seeds, for the seeds are destined to grow into a new generation of plants. Why is it desirable for a plant to spread its seeds widely? Try to work out possible reasons, then turn to the next chapter.

Nine

Fruits and dispersal

Have you ever tried growing cress for eating? Perhaps you sowed the seeds on wet blotting-paper, or on a damp piece of flannel, but no doubt you sowed them thickly in order to get the dense mass of shoots which we eat. Such crowded conditions are not good for the growth of plants – many become starved and eventually die, while in nature many others are eaten by animals such as slugs. Charles Darwin recorded how he cleared and dug a little plot of earth 3 feet by 2 feet, and marked every seedling that came up. 357 seedlings appeared, but only 62 survived; most of the others were eaten off.

If all the seeds from one plant fell to the ground immediately underneath and around the parent, they would be in competition with one another and with the parent for light, as well as for the water and mineral salts available in the soil. There would be a great risk of mass destruction by animals, and of the rapid spread of any kind of disease which affected that kind of plant. Hence there are strong advantages to be gained by efficient spreading of the seeds over a wider area, even though many of them may in fact fall into unsuitable places.

Dispersal methods

One warm, sunny afternoon I was sitting at my laboratory bench when there was a sudden sharp sound of something hitting the window, but on looking round I could find no obvious cause. When it happened a second time I was more fortunate; a small round object was still rolling along the

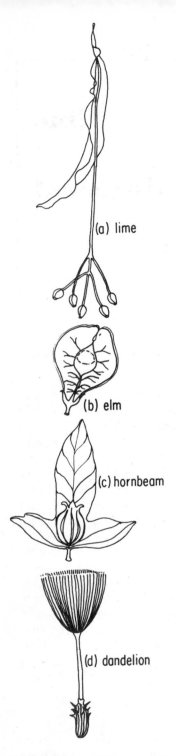

(a) lime

(b) elm

(c) hornbeam

(d) dandelion

Fig. 26 Some wind-dispersed fruits. The first three all have a dry papery wing, but dandelion has a parachute of silky hairs

bench beside the window. On examination it turned out to be a ripe seed of the everlasting pea plant. Some stems of this, complete with ripening pods, had been brought into the room, and left standing in a jar of water. The hot sun had completed the drying of the pods to the point at which the shrinking sides had suddenly torn apart, and had twisted violently, firing out the seeds, which had travelled about 10 feet and would have gone further still but for the window panes.

Such an 'explosion' is but one of the numerous ways in which a plant may disperse its seeds; similar mechanisms are found in garden peas and beans, as well as in wild plants such as gorse. Not all 'explosive' or 'splitting' fruits do so by drying out. I am always fascinated by the squirting cucumber, a plant with fruits about two inches long which become so filled with juice that the slightest touch causes them to discharge a bitter-tasting fluid, and with it the small seeds. If you ever try to grow them (although not native to Britain, they will grow and fruit outdoors in the summer)*, don't bend too closely over plants with ripe fruits!

A great variety of plants make use of the wind to spread their seeds abroad. A few illustrations of examples are shown in Fig. 26. This method is common among trees, where their height helps by holding the fruits right up in the wind currents. Examine as many as you can of these fruits:

> Ash, elm, sycamore, lime, old man's beard (clematis), dandelion, and thistle.

What features do they have in common? Consider their weight, and their shape. Stand out in a breeze and make several trials – say 5 each – with different types, and find out the average distance each fruit travels when released from a standard height.

The antirrhinum and the poppy also make use of wind, but in a different way. Take a ripe fruit and sway it from side to side, so imitating the action of the wind. We call this the censer method of dispersal. How do the seeds escape? What do you notice about the seeds – number, size?

Our third group of fruits include those of burdock, goosegrass, avens and agrimony. All these are plants of waysides – the verges of country roads, paths through woods, or beside hedges. Examine their fruits closely. All have some kind of hook device. No doubt you have had to remove goosegrass from your trousers or socks after a walk through rough grass or hedgesides, or have used the burrs of a burdock for throwing at other people's clothes. In nature these fruits catch on the furry coats of animals and are carried along until they get

* Obtainable from Messrs. Thompson & Morgan, of Ipswich.

brushed off. You will find that a variety of structures are used to provide hooks. Can you spot from where the hooks come in avens and goosegrass?

Next we think of those fruits which are attractive and edible; like a cherry, or a tomato. Here are some questions to answer about them:

1. Such fruits must not be eaten before the seeds inside are ripe, or they will be useless. How is this avoided?

2. To have a good chance of being eaten, a fruit must be easily spotted. How is this achieved?

3. It must be pleasant to eat. What part of the fruit satisfies this requirement?

4. The seed must not be damaged when the fruit is eaten, so it must be protected in some way. One way is by having a bulky layer which can't be swallowed whole or easily chewed. The other is by a layer which resists the attack of the animal's digestive juices, so that the seeds pass out unharmed with the dung. Which method is used by a cherry, which by a tomato?

Find out for yourself two other examples of edible fruits and work out the answers for them, too.

There are some other ways, less common, used by plants to assist seed dispersal. Use your school library, or your local public library to find out more about them.

Lastly, here is a piece of practical work to show the effect of seed dispersal. Carefully clear a small patch of ground, say about one foot by one foot. Leave it bare for four weeks. How many seedlings have appeared? How many recognisably different forms are there? If you have the time and opportunity you can keep watch on them over a long period, to see how many of these seedlings manage to survive, and how many kinds are successful in the competition for survival.

Pass by a country roadside, with its accompanying hedge, at any time in the summer months, and you can hardly fail to notice the vigorous growth of many different plants, or the sight and sound of animal life. Come that way again in winter; where now are the springing stems, the multitude of leaf and flower shapes, or the moving variety of creatures? Where have they gone? Another way of framing such a question would be to ask what is the effect of the short daylight and low temperatures of the winter season.

Experiment 23. How does temperature affect the growth of seedlings?

Take several tubes and place in each some well-dampened cotton wool. Add six cress seeds to each, put a loose cotton wool plug in the neck of each tube, and leave in a warm place until the seedling shoots have appeared. Then place the tubes in different temperatures, such as a greenhouse, a warm room, a cold room, outside. All tubes will need to receive similar amounts of light, and the cotton wool in the tube must be kept moist. After 7 days, remove the seedlings and measure the shoots. Work out an average length for each group. Does a lowering of temperature slow down growth? What would happen if still lower temperatures occurred?

Experiment 24. What effect does temperature have on the activity of blowfly maggots?

Take several glass dishes with lids (not airtight) and put in each ten maggots. Place the dishes in different temperatures, ranging from near 0°C (surround the dish with some crushed ice) to about 40°C (a controlled temperature oven could be used). Compare the amount of activity shown by the maggots in each group. Do low temperatures reduce activity?

If each dish is provided with a little raw meat the experiment can be kept going for two-three days. Observe daily. When fully grown the maggot forms a pupa inside a hard brown case. Compare the numbers of pupae found on successive days in each dish. Does temperature affect growth rate as measured by time of pupa formation?

The woody frames of bush and tree are still in the hedgerow, of course, and underneath lie the rotting heaps of their fallen leaves. Bushes and trees are called *woody perennials*. Perennial means that they live for a number of years, at the very least more than two years. A woody plant is one which forms permanent stems of woody material. Most of those found in British hedgerows are of the kind described as *deciduous*, which means that they shed all their leaves at the same time of the year, which in our climate is in autumn. Look on the branches for the scar left behind where each leaf fell off. Above that scar is a bud, from which the new growth will begin next spring. Both the buds and the live cells of the branches themselves need protection against winter weather. The branches are clothed in bark, made up of dead cells with corky walls. To see how the tender young leaves and flower buds for next year are protected we can dissect a bud.

Unfortunately for our present purpose the buds of many hedgerow bushes and trees are rather too small to be easily examined, so it may be more convenient to illustrate the point by using the large bud of the horse chestnut. What do you notice from the outside? Around the bud are numbers of bud scales. They are arranged in pairs, the two scales of a pair being on opposite sides of the bud. Note all the observable features of this pair – colour, stickiness and shape, for instance – then remove them. Do the same with the next pair. Continue until all the scales have been removed. How many pairs are there? What changes in appearance have you found? When you get to the tiny folded leaves and flower buds, what extra protection have they?

Not all woody perennials lose their leaves in the autumn. *Evergreens* such as holly, laurel, or pine, have thick leaves with much wax on the surfaces, especially the upper surface, where it produces a very shiny appearance. Privet, which grows in field hedges in areas with chalky soils, has rather thick leaves of this kind, and loses them only slowly through the winter. The wax layer reduces the amount of water loss from the leaves, and this is important to evergreens since in winter the cold soil hinders the uptake of water by roots. Strange as it may seem, plants can suffer from water shortage in the winter! The leaves of evergreens may last for several years, being shed a few at a time in late spring or summer.

What of the soft green plants so abundant under and around a hedge? There are three places where we can look for clues, one of them being in the litter of dead leaves and other debris at ground level. Collect some handfuls of this material and take them back to the laboratory. When you sort through this very carefully you should have some interesting finds. Among them may well be the remains of fruits, or individual seeds. How many different kinds can you recognise? You could try germinating some in a box of moist soil put in a warm place. How many different forms of seedlings appear? The longer you can leave the box the better, for not all the seeds will start to grow straightaway. Some, in fact, like those of the wild rose, require a period of exposure to cold weather before they will grow.

Some of the seeds you have found may have come from the hedge bushes, as in the case of haw stones dropped by birds feeding on the red fruits of hawthorn, but others may be from plants which survive winter only in the form of seeds. In such a case, the plant completes its growth in one season, flowers, sets and disperses its seeds, and then dies. Such a plant is termed an *annual*. Many garden weeds have this sort of life pattern, as for instance shepherd's purse and groundsel. Two annual plants which occur widely at roadsides are common vetch, a member of the pea family, and red deadnettle.

Also in your collection of litter there are quite likely to be animal forms; we will consider them later.

Our second point of search is among the clumps of deadgrass leaves and those of neighbouring plants. Collect samples of any animals you find, and look for live green shoots hidden and protected under the dead leaves. Many grasses are *perennials*, but they are *herbaceous*, that is, herb-like, with soft green parts, not woody ones. By autumn the older leaves are dying off, but they remain on the plant through the winter. Can you find other examples of this habit?

If it is possible to do so, dig a hole in the soil by or near a hedge. This will give you a chance to look for animals and plants which overwinter beneath the soil surface. Fig. 24 shows some examples of plants which do this. Have you found any of these, or others like them?

Sometimes the underground part is a thick upright root, as in burdock, jack-by-the-hedge, or a number of plants known as hedge parsley. These are *biennials*, plants whose life extends over two years (Fig. 27(a)). When such a plant grows from

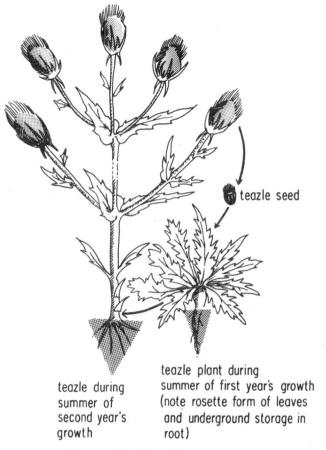

teazle seed

teazle during
summer of
second year's
growth

teazle plant during
summer of first year's growth
(note rosette form of leaves
and underground storage in
root)

Fig. 27 (a)   Biennial life cycle

seed it produces leaves during the first spring and summer
and in the autumn dies down to its underground storage organ.
Next spring the plant uses the food stored in its fleshy root in
making rapid growth, and flowers soon form. When the seeds
are ripe and have been dispersed, the plant is exhausted and
dies.

In other cases the underground part is a special stem. Some
examples of hedgerow plants with these underground stems
are shown in Fig. 27 (a) and (b), but there are many others.
Wild arum or cuckoo-pint has a short and fat underground
stem, of a type called a corm. The buried stems of bracken and
white deadnettle are longer, thinner and run horizontally.
They are called rhizomes. Why do we call these structures
stems when they are found below ground? If you have been
able to collect some of these, examine them for the possession of
buds and the scars of leaves. Only stems bear leaves and buds.

Another type of underground storage organ is the bulb.
Bluebell, which in some areas of Britain is found in hedgerows,
although it is much better known as a woodland plant, has

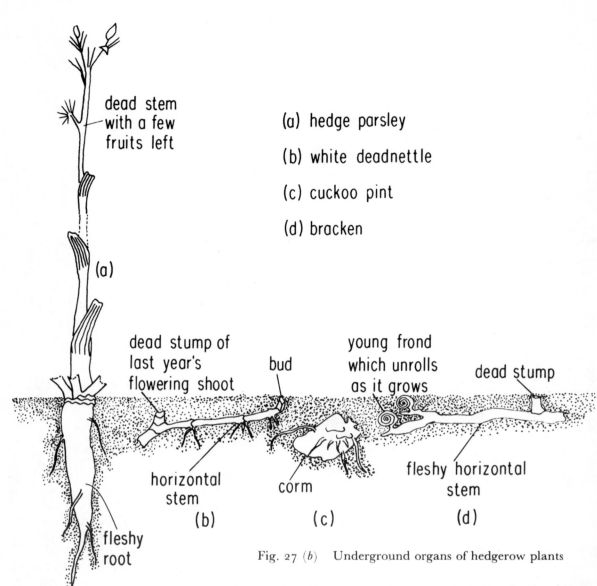

dead stem
with a few
fruits left

(a) hedge parsley

(b) white deadnettle

(c) cuckoo pint

(d) bracken

(a)

dead stump of
last year's
flowering shoot

bud

young frond
which unrolls
as it grows

dead stump

horizontal
stem

(b)

corm

(c)

fleshy horizontal
stem

(d)

fleshy
root

Fig. 27 (*b*)   Underground organs of hedgerow plants

a bulb and so does crow garlic, an onion-like plant. To see the structure of a bulb, it is convenient to cut in halves a tulip or onion bulb. Can you see at the centre the tender young foliage leaves and flower-bud for next spring's growth? Note also the white fleshy scale-leaves which make up most of the bulb (see Fig. 28).

If the new year's growth is to come from such an underground organ, we might expect to find that it contains stored food for this growth. Since starch is so common a stored food in plants, the iodine solution test is the obvious one to try on slices cut from the specimens you have found. In cases where

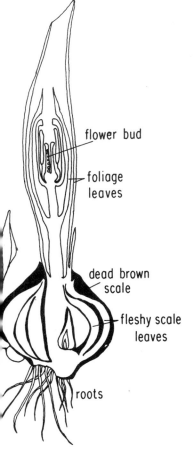

28 Structure of a tulip bulb halved vertically, after it has begun to grow out

flower bud

foliage leaves

dead brown scale

fleshy scale leaves

roots

a negative result is given, you could try the Fehling's test for sugars. Record your results.

Animal Survival

We have seen that as the temperature of their surroundings falls, so insects become less and less active. This is true for all the 'cold-blooded' animals, those whose body temperature varies with that of the surroundings. Only birds and mammals, the 'warm-blooded' animals, maintain a constant body temperature and so can remain active in cold weather. In cold conditions, however, warm-blooded animals lose much heat to the cold outside air, and must consume more food to keep up their body temperature. If the food they eat is of a kind which becomes scarce in winter, then they must have some way of overcoming this difficulty.

No doubt you know that a number of the birds we see in summer, such as the swallow, which feeds on flying insects, migrate in early autumn to warmer climates. If such birds remained here in winter, they would not find their summer food available. It is perhaps less well-known that other birds, such as lapwing, move southwards or coastwards without leaving the British Isles. Yet other birds, such as blackbird or thrush, remain in their usual areas and can be seen hunting in the hedgerow for their varied diet of worms, snails, grubs and berries. In winter they are joined by birds which migrate here from colder climates further north. Two of these you may see searching for food in the hedges during the cold months are the fieldfare and the redwing.

A fieldfare is similar in size and shape to a thrush, but has a distinctive grey head and rump (the part of the back just in front of the tail). The rest of the back is chestnut brown, the wings and tail dark brown, and the breast is speckled like our song thrush, but with very dark brown marks. The redwing is also similar in size and appearance to a song thrush, but there is a reddish patch on the side of the body above the legs, and a light stripe over the eye.

Unable to fly, mammals cannot migrate to warmer lands. In searching under your hedge, you may find a hedgehog, curled up with prickles outwards, among a mass of dead grass and leaves. He is in a state of hibernation, a long sleep during which his heart beats very slowly and his breathing rate is hardly noticeable. The fat he stored in his body during the late summer and autumn provides food for this period, during which he could not obtain his normal diet of insects.

Field mice make nests inside holes in the ground, quite often in the soil of hedgebanks, and store food in them for their winter use.

Far more numerous than the mammals and birds in our hedge, and the road verge beside it, are many kinds of cold-blooded animals. These will spend the winter in an inactive state although some, like slugs, may emerge from their shallow burrows on milder days and crawl around in search of food. For instance, the catch of animals that you made while searching the dead leaves and so on will surely include snails. Inspect one closely. How does the snail close the opening in its shell?

Have you found any earthworms while digging in the soil? Were any found coiled up in an enlarged part of their burrow?

Insects form a major part of the animal population and we can find quite a number of these, at various stages of life, even in the winter time. Table 3 shows just a few of the possible finds. In addition to these, the winter eggs of aphids can often be found in clusters of tiny round objects in the crevices of bark. The lackey moth lays eggs in a collar around a twig of a bush such as wild rose. Some other more-or-less familiar animals to look for are wood-lice, centipedes, millipedes, and spiders, but I won't tell you in advance where these may be. Find out for yourself! When you have finished examining the animals, don't just leave them to die of neglect. Unless you can keep them in suitable conditions similar to those in nature, return them to where you found them.

Table 3. Insects of the Winter Hedgerow

Name of Insect	Stage in Winter	Place where they might be found	Appearance
Earwig	Adult	In nest of dead plant fragments. Often in pairs	
Wasp	Adult queen	Crevice or small hole	Striped black and yellow
Humble Bee	Adult queen	Crevice or small hole	Hairy, squat, striped orange and black
Privet Hawk moth	Pupa	In soil in areas where Privet occurs	About $1\frac{1}{2}''$ long Smooth, brown
Cinnabar moth	Pupa	In soil	$\frac{1}{2}''$ long. Reddish
Ghost swift moth	Larva (Caterpillar)	In soil, among grass roots	$1\frac{1}{2}''$ long. White with brown head
Hedge brown butterfly	Caterpillar	At base of grass tufts	$\frac{3}{4}''$ Slug-shaped, with two-lobed head Pale yellow or pale green

Eleven

Life springs anew

Plants vary enormously in the number of seeds they produce. The double coconut palm of the Seychelles Islands bears not more than a dozen fruits at a time and each one spends ten years developing on the tree before it is ready to fall. The foxglove, on the other hand, is a plant which lives for two years, but produces perhaps forty fruits each with a very large number of seeds, so that the plant's total seed production may reach half a million. What a difference in size there is! The double coconut fruit weighs 40 pounds, a great deal of this weight being that of the large coconut, which is the seed. The fruit is dispersed by ocean currents. The dust-like seeds of foxglove are sprinkled like pepper from the openings in the fruit when the wind sways the stalk. In both cases, some seeds will be wasted because they arrive at unsuitable places, or start to grow at unfavourable times, but enough will survive to provide a new generation of plants.

We have already seen how the production of seeds is one way in which a plant can overcome the hazards of winter, or the dry season of hotter countries. Often, however, at the time when the seeds are shed conditions are still quite good. Why is it that when seeds fall to the earth they do not start to grow, to *germinate*, and produce new plants there and then? In some cases they do, but many of the seedlings become casualties later when conditions are bad; in others the seed has built-in mechanisms to prevent premature growth.

Lupins, in common with many others among the family of plants called legumes, have seeds with a very tough and waterproof seed coat. This coat breaks down very slowly in the soil, and only then can growth begin. The seeds of apple and peach will only start to grow after they have been exposed to several weeks of near-freezing temperatures, such as would occur during winter. This mechanism reduces the risk of young seedlings being exposed to severe weather after germinating in autumn or in a mild winter spell. Tomato seeds inside the juicy pulp of the fruit do not grow there because the juice contains chemicals which prevent germination. Similar chemicals occur in the seed coats of many desert plants, and only a heavy downfall of rain is sufficient to wash them away. This prevents growth beginning after a slight shower, insufficient to permit continued survival.

Apart from such special factors, seeds have certain basic requirements if they are to germinate. Our first task in this section is to investigate the nature of these requirements.

Experiment 25. To investigate the conditions needed for the germination of cress seeds.

Take a set of four small bottles or wide-mouthed tubes, and treat them as follows (Fig. 29):

Tube (*a*). Put in some wetted cotton-wool or sawdust, and a number – say six – of cress or other small seeds. These seeds can obtain moisture from the cotton wool, they have the gases of air available, and the tube should be put in a warm place.

Tube (*b*). Set up in the same way as (*a*), with the same number

Fig. 29   Experiment on conditions needed for germination of seeds

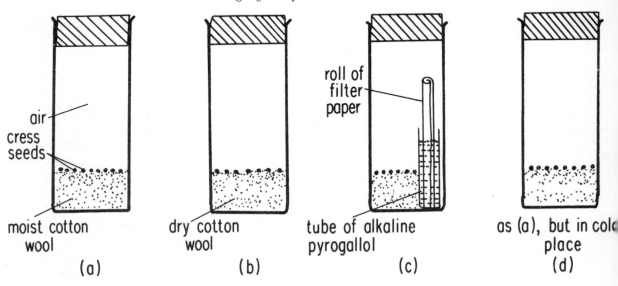

of seeds, but with the important difference that the cotton wool is to be left dry. These seeds will have the same conditions as those in (a), except that they will have no water.

Tube (c). This tube is to have wet cotton wool with the seeds, but there is to be a smaller tube containing a solution known as alkaline pyrogallol, set upright inside the tube with the seeds. Care must be taken in handling this reagent, since it contains sodium hydroxide, which burns the skin, as well as damaging seeds. Alkaline pyrogallol is used to remove the oxygen from air; it will be more effective in this experiment if a piece of filter paper is dipping into the solution (see Fig. 29). When you have completed the assembly of this tube place it with (a) and (b) in a warm spot.

Tube (d). Set up as for (a), but leave in a cold place, such as the bottom of a refrigerator, where the temperature is a little above freezing.

After several days – one week will do very well – examine all the tubes. In which has growth occurred? How do you account for the absence of growth in the others? What does this experiment tell us about the conditions necessary for germination?

You will notice that we have not considered whether light is needed for germination. How could you investigate this point? Practical studies indicate that, while many seeds do not require light for germination to occur, there are some kinds which do not germinate unless exposed to light, such as mistletoe and some varieties of lettuce. On the other hand, there are some seeds which will only germinate in darkness, such as onion and many lilies. In every case, however, light becomes essential for all seedlings, as can be shown by this experiment.

Experiment 26. To compare the growth of seedlings in light and darkness.

Germinate two equal sets of seeds, using the knowledge gained from your previous experiment, and put both sets in a warm place. Whereas one set will be exposed to good light, the other set is to be enclosed in a dark box. Examine the sets after 7–10 days and list the differences between the seedlings. Consider stem length and thickness, leaf size, and leaf colour.

The type of growth which occurs when seedlings are allowed to grow in darkness is described as etiolation. Try the effect of making a small hole in one side of your dark box. If etiolated seedlings do not soon reach a lighted region they will die. Can you explain this, using information gained from your studies of plant nutrition?

We may say then, that light is needed for the healthy growth of seedlings; so, in fact, are various mineral salts which the root hairs of the seedling would normally obtain from the soil. Although seeds may be germinated on damp cotton wool or filter paper, the plants that arise will not live for long unless moved into soil or some prepared material containing the necessary salts.

Structure of a Seed

Take a few large seeds, such as those of the runner bean (or broad bean) and soak them in water overnight. They will swell up and become softer, making examination of their structure easier.

First look at the seed coat, the testa, and find the scar left where the seed was attached to the ovary wall. This scar is called the hilum, and if you squeeze the seed gently you will see a tiny drop of water emerge from a very small hole by one end of it. This hole is the micropyle, through which the pollen tube entered the ovule during the process of fertilisation. Now peel away the testa and you will see that under a slight bulge near the micropyle there is a triangular-shaped radicle, the first root of the plant. The bulk of the seed is made up of the two cotyledons, hidden between which is a tiny shoot, called the plumule. Can you see two minute leaves attached to the plumule? Notice, too, that each cotyledon is attached by a short stalk to a very short region, the hypocotyl, which links the radicle and the plumule into one continuous structure (see Fig. 30).

The cotyledons are food-stores; chop up parts of one and find out whether starch is present.

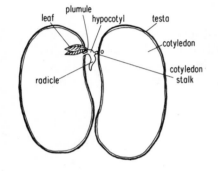

Fig. 30 Structure of an opened runner bean seed

The Course of Germination

If you plant several of your runner beans in damp sawdust, you can remove them one at a time every 3 days to watch the progress of germination. You should make drawings to show the major stages.

First of all, water is taken up through the micropyle and the testa, with consequent swelling of the seed. This water dissolves substances present in the seed which when in solution attack the stored starch, breaking it down to sugars. These substances are examples of *enzymes*, which are catalysts of a type found in all living things; their rate of work increases as temperature rises, up to the point at which the living tissues become damaged by heat. This is one important reason why warmth is necessary for good germination. The sugars produced from the starch are used to make building materials and also to provide energy, through respiration, for growth.

The expansion of the radicle splits the testa, the radicle emerges and grows downwards in the soil. Soon afterwards, the plumule appears from between the cotyledons and begins to grow upwards towards the surface. Notice the hook-shaped tip of the plumule. Why do you think it has this shape? What happens to the bent portion after the plumule has grown up above ground level?

By the time the first leaves begin to expand the radicle has produced side (lateral) roots and on these can be seen the root hairs, which are absorbing water and mineral salts from the soil. The plant is now able to fend for itself, using its green leaves to carry out photosynthesis. The cotyledons have shrivelled up, as they have lost all their stored food, and have no further function.

Further Practical Work

Examine other types of seeds and study their germination, e.g. dwarf bean, sunflower or cress. In these examples the cotyledons are pushed up above the ground surface by the hypocotyl becoming much longer; in sunflower and cress the cotyledons then become the first pair of green leaves.

Twelve

The variety of life — sorting it out

When we began our study of biology we considered the characteristic activities of living things and the way in which mammals and flowering plants live. As a result we were able to note some ways in which plants and animals differ. Do you remember the main points?

1. A plant is able to make all the foodstuffs it needs from simple substances present in air and soil, with the aid of energy from light. An animal must eat ready-made food, taken from plants or from other animals.

2. Animals require to move about to find their food – movement is a characteristic of animals. Plants remain in one place, anchored to it by their roots.

3. To be easily moveable, an animal's body must be quite compact, but in a plant a spreading habit is an advantage. Spread-out stems and leaves give the best exposure to light, and spread-out roots help in obtaining water and salts, as well as providing anchorage.

4. Animals grow all over their bodies, but plants grow only from the tips of stems and roots.

These are general statements. Are they always true? Consider the following examples, preferably by looking at actual specimens, but otherwise by inspection of the pictures in Fig. 31.

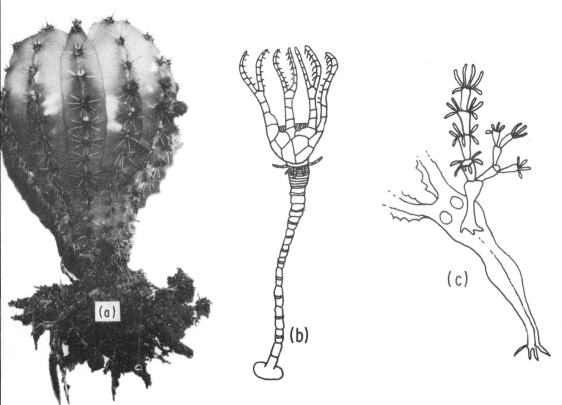

Fig. 31   Some organisms which are not typically animal- or plant-like. (*a*) *Echinocactus*. (*b*) Sea lily. (*c*) Sea fir, attached to seaweed. (*d*) Mushroom. (*e*) Venus' flytrap. (*f*) Sea anemone. (Not on same scale.)

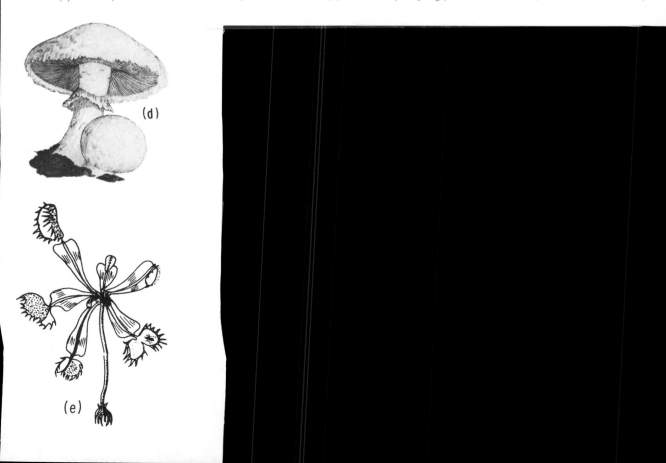

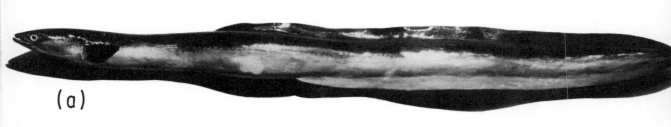

(a)

Fig. 32   Some aquatic animals. (a) Eel. (b) Starfish. (c) Sea lily. (d) Sea squirt. (e) Peacock worm. (f) Ragworm. (g) Acorn worm. (h) Sea cucumber. (Not on the same scale.)

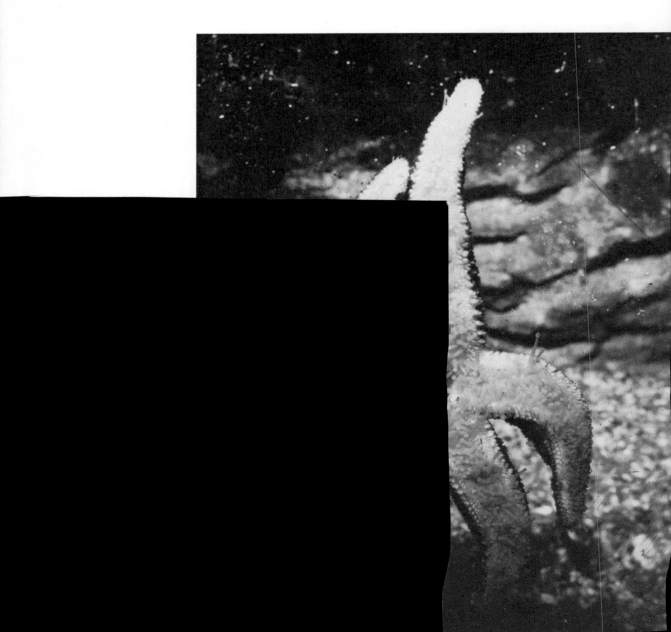

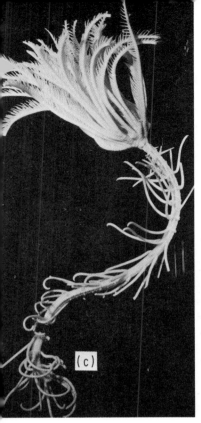

(c)

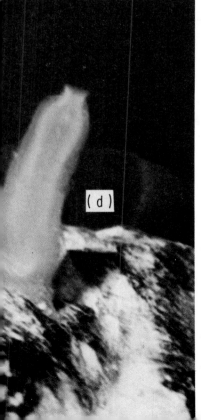

(d)

Each of these differs from the usual standard of plant or animal in at least one major particular. In each case, too, the difference is related to some important aspect of the organism's way of life. For example, a sea anemone spreads out its tentacles in the water, while the rest of the body remains stationary, and uses them to catch small fish or other animals as they swim past. In all other respects each one can be seen clearly to 'belong' to the animal or the plant kingdom, as when a cactus is observed to possess chlorophyll, to remain in one place and to have a spread-out root system.

When the biologist turns his attention to some of the organisms so small that they can only be seen with a microscope, then he may find it impossible to say with conviction either 'animal' or 'plant'. Fig. 36 (page 73) shows a small organism called *Euglena viridis*, which sometimes occurs in freshwater puddles in such vast numbers as to give the water a greenish tint, although a single specimen is so small that the 400x magnification on the microscope shows only a few of its features. This organism has a compact body, and can swim about actively, but it manufactures its food by photosynthesis. Related organisms are in some cases more animal-like, and in others more plant-like. Other micro-organisms show even less resemblance to our general pattern of plant and animal. Many people consider that it is better to regard these as a third kingdom, that of the Protists, a practice which we shall follow.

Having recognised the three main groupings or kingdoms, we can hardly be content to stop at this point. Each kingdom contains a bewildering variety of forms of life; further subdivision is essential, but brings problems of its own. Fig. 32 shows us a number of animals, all of which live under water. Here again, it would be best if we could look at actual specimens of them, but the diagrams are better than nothing. What visible characteristics could be used to sort them out?

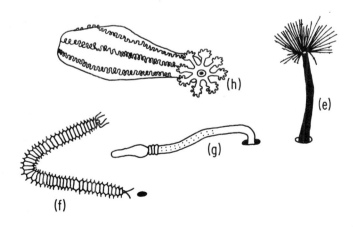

(h)

(e)

(g)

(f)

Consider body shape. What main types can be recognised? An alternative would be to divide the specimens into those with armlike structures, tentacles, and those without.

Both of these characteristics are closely linked with the way in which their possessors live. Animals which remain anchored in one spot often have tentacles with which they can sieve the water to obtain food, tentacles radiating outwards like the spokes of a wheel. Actively moving animals would be handicapped by such spreading structures, but can go in search of food; such animals usually have a long and relatively narrow body. If we study the internal construction of our chosen examples, this gives us a quite different picture of their kinships. We find for instance that the starfish, the sea lily and the sea cucumber are related; the eel, the acorn worm and the sea squirt are placed in the same group; the peacock worm and the ragworm, although feeding in very different ways, have closely similar internal organs. So it is that by a full study of both external and internal features, and sometimes of the young form as well as the adult, that a classification of living things must be built. Fig. 33 shows part of the result.

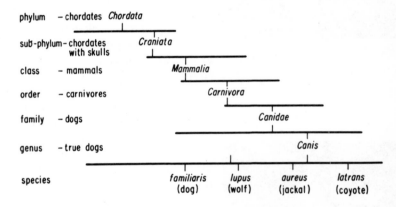

Fig. 33   Part of a classification of living things

In this scheme, each group possesses all the basic characters of those above it in the table, but has some special features of its own. At the lower levels, the members may be so closely similar that they are given the same name in everyday language, as in buttercups, or oaks. A look at a domestic dog, a fox, a wolf, and a jackal soon convinces us that they are closely related; the fact that they and seals, and kangaroos, are all mammals is a less obvious one.

While we are considering the range of life we shall be mainly concerned with the large units of classification, such as the *Phyla* (the plural of *Phylum*). At the bottom of our table, however, is the species – one individual type of organism.

Each species is given a name which consists of two words, First, the genus name, which it shares with its closest relatives, and then the species name, which applies to it alone, and which often describes some feature of that organism. For example, *albus* or *alba* would indicate that some prominent feature, such as the hair or the petals, was white. Many plants which have been used in medicine are given as a species name the term *officinalis*, while *vulgaris* has its older English meaning of common. Some examples of names are given in Table 4. The two-name system was first used by Linnaeus, a great figure in the history of biology. Linnaeus, a Swedish naturalist, lived in the eighteenth century, and used his extensive knowledge of plants to devise a system of plant classification.

Table 4. Some Species Names

Genus name	Species name	English name
Apis	*mellifica* (honey-maker)	Honey bee
Bellis	*perennis* (perennial)	Daisy
Pinus	*sylvestris* (lives in woods)	Scots pine
Aesculus	*hippocastanum* (hippo = horse castanum = chestnut)	Horse chestnut
Lumbricus	*terrestris* (of the earth)	Earthworm
Homo	*sapiens* (wise)	Man

The serious student of biology can soon learn to place a specimen in the phylum and the class to which it belongs, but will very often need the help of printed guides and 'keys' to carry the identification further, down to the level of the species. A key is a list of questions to each of which there are two (occasionally more) possible answers. The right answer is found by examining the specimen, and this leads to another question, and so on until the identity is tracked down. Refer to Fig. 34. Here are four (imaginary) animals with the same general structure. Suppose I was not familiar with these four types, but had found a specimen which was like one or other of them. The key might go like this:

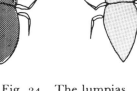

Fig. 34 The lumpias

69

Question Number	Possible answers	Refer to Question Number, or Name
1.	Are the feelers long or short?	
	Short	2
	Long	3
2.	What colour is the body?	
	Black . .	*Lumpia alpha*
	Grey . . .	*Lumpia beta*
3.	Is the animal of one colour, or striped?	
	Striped . .	*Lumpia gamma*
	One colour .	*Lumpia delta*

In constructing a key, a biologist makes much use of the apparently minor differences which distinguish one genus from another, and one species from others in the same genus.

Let us try this out for ourselves. Consider the buttercups. These belong to the family of flowering plants called the *Ranunculaceae*, and to the genus *Ranunculus*. This genus includes not only the plants we call buttercups, but also aquatic plants called crowfoots, waterside-loving spearworts, and an inhabitant of damp ground, the lesser celandine. They are all soft green plants, their flowers having 5 sepals, 5 separate petals, many stamens and many single-seeded carpels (the lesser celandine, however has 11 structures which cannot clearly be distinguished as sepals or petals). Of the buttercups, 3 are widespread in Britain, while a fourth is nowadays a much less common weed of cornfields. The 3 common ones are illustrated in Fig. 35. They all fit in with our mental picture of a buttercup, yet have clear and consistent differences. Can you spot any of these from the drawings and accompanying descriptions?

Fig. 35 also shows a spearwort, a water crowfoot, and a lesser celandine. Assume that these, together with the three buttercups in the previous Figure are the only members of the genus *Ranunculus*, and devise a key which would enable you to identify a specimen as belonging to one of these 6 species. When you have tried this, you may like to refer to the key for the genus *Ranunculus* given in a flora of the British Isles, such as Clapham, Tutin and Warburg's *Excursion Flora of the British Isles*, published by Cambridge University Press, or Makins' *Concise Flora of Great Britain*, published by Oxford University Press.

Having gained some idea of the principles of classification, it is now appropriate for us to look at the major groups into which living things are sorted.

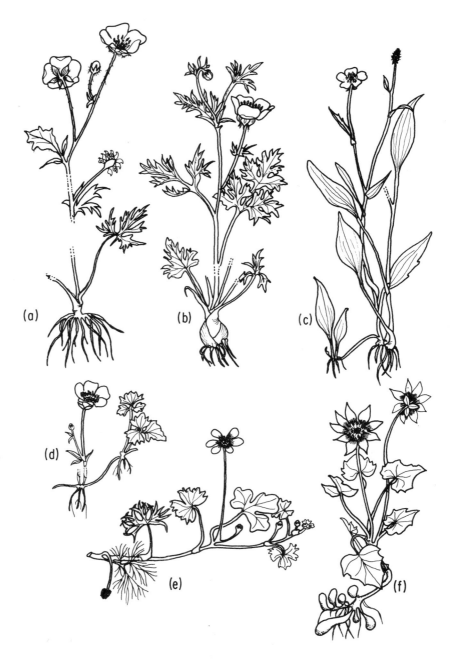

Fig. 35 Members of the genus *Ranunculus*. (*a*) *Ranunculus acris*, the acrid buttercup. (*b*) *R. bulbosus*, the bulbous buttercup. (*c*) *R. flammula*, the spearwort. (*d*) *R. repens*, the creeping buttercup. (*e*) *R. aquatilis*, the water crowfoot. (*f*) *R. ficaria*, the lesser celandine

Thirteen

Neither plant nor animal — the Protists

One sometimes sees coloured pictures showing the wild life of a region or a type of countryside, with animals resting on every branch and occupying every square yard or so of the ground! While showing us as many different creatures as he can, the artist often conveys an impression which is false in at least two important ways. These animals are often largely birds or mammals, which are at the upper end of the size scale of life, and they are never really so closely packed together!

In fact, for every single bird or mammal, there are countless hosts of smaller, less obvious organisms. Some we only notice when they bite or sting us, others we cannot even see without the aid of a powerful microscope. Many of these minute forms of life play vital roles in the cycle of nature, breaking down dead bodies and returning their chemicals to circulation, such as the 'nitrifying bacteria' in the soil which produce nitrates needed by green plants. Some we harness to our use, such as the bacteria which give flavour to cheese, while others can invade our bodies and cause disease, such as those producing malaria or sleeping sickness.

Among these minute forms of life, the terms plant and animal cannot really be applied, and we use the general term Protists. One such organism is Euglena, an inhabitant of puddles and larger areas of freshwater. You won't be able to see it, though, unless you have a powerful microscope available, for even at 400x magnification one can only see a slim green shape propelling itself across the slide. Fig. 36 shows the appearance of this organism as revealed at still higher magnifications.

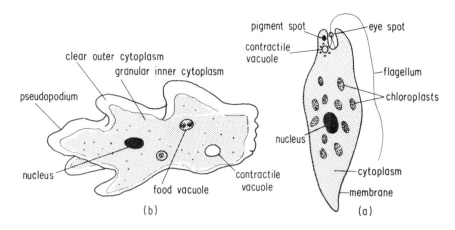

Fig. 36   Protists.   (*a*) Amoeba   (*b*) *Euglena.*

From this diagram you can see that the minute body is not divided up into separate cells (Chapter 3, p. 11), but there is a nucleus and there is cytoplasm. The green colour suggests the presence of chlorophyll and will tell us that here is an organism which is able to carry out photosynthesis. Since Euglena lives in water, it cannot get its carbon dioxide directly from the air, but from that dissolved in the water, and the mineral salts it needs also come from the water.

If some water containing many Euglena is put in a tube covered with dark paper, apart from a small hole on one side, soon the Euglenas all collect around this lighted patch. They are able to detect the direction of light by the working of the eye-spot, and are able to swim towards light by the beating of the whip-like flagellum. Euglena can get all the oxygen it needs for respiration through its body surface, and any waste substances to be excreted pass out through the surface. There is a tendency for more water than is needed to leak in: the function of the contractile vacuole is to bale it out. The contractile vacuole slowly fills with water until it reaches full size, then it discharges the water to the outside.

When Euglena has grown by steady enlargement to a full size, it reproduces – by splitting in half. First the nucleus divides into two equal parts, and then the body starts to divide at the front end, the split extending backwards until there are two separate daughter Euglenas. We call this method of reproducing *binary fission.*

In which respects is Euglena rather plant-like? In what ways is it more like an animal? Use the information given to make out two sets of resemblances, one to animals, one to plants. You may well conclude that it is impossible to say for certain whether it should be called one or the other.

If you put a sample of pond water under the microscope, it

frequently shows a variety of forms more-or-less similar to Euglena. Some of these appear to be more like typical plants and are often grouped by botanists among the Algae (see Chapter 20), while others do not have chlorophyll but do capture and digest solid food, behaviour which is animal-like. For this reason these latter forms are often included in the zoologist's classification of animals as Protozoa, first 'animals'.

Protozoa

Amoeba is not, as some books suggest, a common fresh-water organism, to be found crawling on the mud in almost any pond. It is, however, one of the largest of the Protozoans, and can be cultured fairly easily in laboratories, so every student of biology soon makes its acquaintance. It is big enough to be just visible to the naked eye as a white speck. It can be seen very well with a junior microscope. Try to identify as many as possible of the features shown in Fig. 36. Notice how many of those features were also present in Euglena. A number of things are missing. What are they? One new structure is present. What is that?

Watching an Amoeba on a microscope slide shows us that it does not swim, but moves by a kind of 'crawling' motion which involves the outflowing of cytoplasm into temporary projections, each called a pseudopodium (literally, a false foot). Amoeba cannot photosynthesise; it must catch food, sometimes smaller living organisms, sometimes pieces of decaying matter. When Amoeba senses food, it surrounds it by pseudopodia and takes it with a drop of water to form a food vacuole. Inside this vacuole the food is attacked by digestive juices, so that it is made available for the Amoeba's use. The processes of respiration, excretion and water control are carried out in the same way as in Euglena, and reproduction is by binary fission.

The Protozoa form an enormous group; some live in fresh and others in sea water, some in the soil, and some in the bodies of larger forms of life. Some examples are shown in Fig. 37. Among the last is one which is a parasite, Plasmodium. A parasite is a living organism which lives in close association with, and at the expense of, another living organism. Plasmodium multiplies inside the human blood cells and liver, causing the disease malaria. This cannot happen unless the parasite is injected into the bloodstream by the bite of a mosquito which has fed some days earlier on the blood of an already infected person. Malaria is, of course, a very serious disease which can nowadays be combated by special drugs but which still attacks large numbers of people in warmer countries. The World Health Organisation is running a large-scale campaign to wipe it out in many countries.

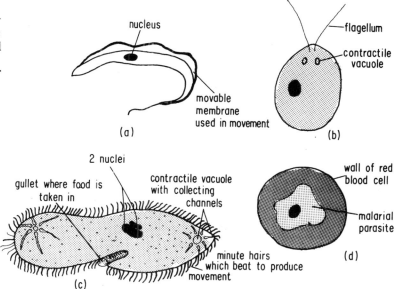

37 Some other Protozoa. (a) *Trypanosoma*. (b) *Polytoma*. (c) *Paramecium*. (d) *Plasmodium*, shown inside red blood cell. *Trypanosoma* and *Plasmodium* are parasitic; the other two are free-living inhabitants of freshwater. *Paramecium* feeds on bacteria, while *Polytoma* absorbs dissolved foodstuffs from declaying matter in the water

Other Protozoan parasites cause the diseases sleeping sickness and amoebic dysentery. Find out in each case the name of the parasite, how it gets into the human body, and the areas of the world where the disease is common.

Something else you might like to do is this: Take a small handful of dried grass and boil it in a pint of water for about 10 minutes. Cool and then leave to stand for two weeks. Take out a little of the brownish, rather unpleasant-smelling water with a pipette, put a drop on a microscope slide, add a coverslip, and then examine under the microscope. You should see more types of Protozoa, some of which you can probably identify by reference to guide books, such as Mellanby's *Animal Life in Fresh Water*, published by Methuen.

Bacteria

If you were to take a spoonful of soil you would be holding in your hand thousands of living creatures. While these would be of many kinds, a large proportion would be bacteria. Bacteria are microscopic organisms, but far smaller than Euglena, the longest reaching about 1/200th of a millimetre. They reproduce by binary fission, and under favourable conditions of food supply and temperature, they can divide as often as every 20 minutes. If this rate was kept up, in 7 hours one bacterium would have produced 2,000,000 descendants. Usually there are not enough food supplies to permit such rapid increase, and in addition many are destroyed by other organisms.

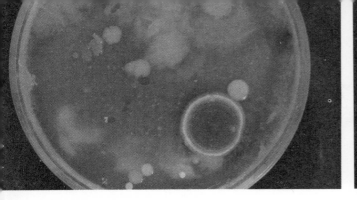 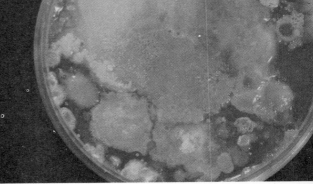

(b)

Fig. 38 Culture plates. (a) Two colonies of mould, one a fluffy mass of colourless threads at the top left, the other a green disc at the bottom right. There are many smaller colonies of bacteria. (b) This is infected almost entirely by bacteria which have covered almost all the surface. At least five different colours are present, from white to deep red

In the laboratory, bacteria are grown on culture plates of agar, a jelly-like material to which is added suitable food substances, such as meat or potato extract. For the following experiment you will need six of these plates, spread out in flat glass dishes, complete with close-fitting lid (these are known as Petri dishes). Do not take off the lid until you are quite ready to carry out the procedure, and replace the lid as soon as you have finished.

Experiment 27. To investigate the growth of bacteria.

1. Leave the dish unopened. In this way the contents, which have been sterilised during preparation, will remain uncontaminated. To sterilise means to kill off all the living organisms present.

2. Take off the lid and leave the plate exposed to the air for five minutes.

3. Breathe several times on the plate.

4. Place your fingertips gently on the jelly, but avoid breaking the surface of the jelly.

5. Allow a little water from an outdoor source to run gently on to the plate, then pour off.

6. Sprinkle a few particles of fresh, very fine soil over the surface.

Leave all the plates in a warm place (over a warm radiator will do very well) for 4–7 days, and then examine them. We can expect to see two kinds of growth: (a) colonies of bacteria, in the form of white or coloured wet-looking spots, and (b) little masses of tangled threads, usually colourless, but sometimes grey or greenish, which are the bodies of fungi. Fig. 38 shows photographs of two plates prepared by this method.

Count and record the number of colonies of bacteria, as far as you can, on each plate. Do not *touch* the colonies, for some may be harmful. When the plates are finished with, disinfectant will be used to kill off all the bacteria.

What else can we learn from the results? Fig. 38(a) shows that bacteria do not just appear; the food must become contaminated for them to develop. Do they lead us to suggest ways

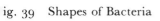

spheres

rods, forming chains

spiral forms with flagella

Fig. 39　Shapes of Bacteria

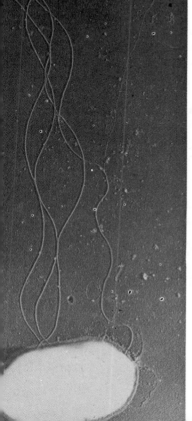

40　Azotobacter magnified
0 times. Note the long strands
toplasm, the flagella, which ex-
from the bacterium. This
ism lives in soil and converts
gen from air into compounds
which green plants can use

in which human food might become infected by harmful bacteria? Examine the results from the other plates. What plain rules for hygiene follow from this?

Some of the shapes which these minute living organisms possess are shown in Fig. 39, while Fig. 40 is a photograph of the bacterium Azotobacter. Apart from a very few, bacteria lack the power to make their own food; they are either sapro-phytes (organisms which digest dead organic matter) or para-sites (ones which feed on other living bodies). Saprophytic forms can be harmful to man if they produce poisonous wastes in foodstuffs, leading to cases of 'food poisoning'. A number of parasitic bacteria cause dangerous diseases in humans, such as cholera, typhoid, and tetanus. Cholera is usually taken in by mouth through drinking contaminated water, typhoid from food handled by a person carrying the disease, and tetanus through the entry of the bacteria in dirt getting in a wound. Such bacteria multiply speedily in the warmth of the body, and quick medical attention is essential.

These examples underline the importance to us and to society of pure water, clean food, and in the case of diseases like diphtheria and tetanus, the value of immunisation. Im-munisation is the development of resistance to the disease, brought about by injection of killed or greatly weakened organ-isms. The body produces chemicals to destroy these, chemicals which persist in the blood and so are ready to combat any later invasion of live bacteria. Without the artificial develop-ment brought about by immunisation, there would be a very grave likelihood of the bacteria getting a fatal hold on the body before it could build up its counter-attack.

Viruses

Bacteria are minute, but viruses are even smaller and can only be seen with the enormous magnifications of the electron microscope. Viruses can only thrive and reproduce inside the living cells of other organisms, but extracts have been made, and some even crystallised. In general, one can say that viruses behave like living things when growing inside a cell, and like non-living substances when outside the cell.

Examples of viruses which invade human cells, multiply there, and having damaged or destroyed the cell, leave it to invade other cells, are measles, smallpox, poliomyelitis and the common cold. In some cases immunisation methods can help us here, as in the cases of smallpox and polio, but in others they are as yet not effective, as with the common cold.

Not all viruses attack animals, for many types infect plants. The curious stripings of tulip petals which one sometimes sees are the result of virus infection, and tobacco, tomato, and sugar beet can suffer badly from virus attack.

Fourteen

Animals with sting cells

'"Cyanea!" I cried, "Cyanea! Behold the Lion's Mane!"' The strange mass at which I pointed did indeed look like a tangled mass torn from the mane of a lion. It lay upon a rocky shelf some three feet under the water, a curious waving, vibrating, hairy creature with streaks of silver among its yellow tresses. It pulsated with a slow, heavy dilation and contraction'. So Sherlock Holmes came to the solution of the schoolmaster's death while bathing on a peaceful Sussex beach. (*The Case-Book of Sherlock Holmes*. IX. The Adventure of the Lion's Mane.) Fortunately, this fictional encounter is not at all likely to come to life in our experience, although many people know the irritating stings of more common jellyfish.

Any paddler in rock pools will have seen some of the smaller sea anemones in hues of red or green, but many of the more colourful ones are found below low water level. Their names hint at their appearance – names like snakelocks, beadlet, dahlia anemone. These too have sting cells, using them to paralyse and kill small animals which swim or crawl past.

In Bermuda houses are built with blocks of white stone cut from the hilltops. This stone is 'coral rock', derived from the massed skeletons of the corals which abound in the warm waters around the island. In many tropical and sub-tropical areas corals form extensive reefs offshore. The outstanding example of this is the Great Barrier Reef of Australia, which runs for 1,260 miles parallel to the coast of Queensland, separated from it by a channel so wide that Captain Cook sailed for 600 miles along it. He did not even suspect that the

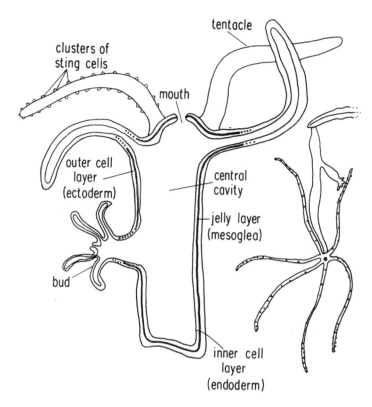

clusters of
sting cells

tentacle

mouth

outer cell
layer
(ectoderm)

central
cavity

jelly layer
(mesoglea)

bud

inner cell
layer
(endoderm)

Fig. 41   Diagram of *Hydra* with a bud

ship was in a channel until it ran aground in a narrower part.

What have these animals – jellyfish, anemone, and coral – in common, enough to justify their being classed in the same phylum, the Coelenterates? They are all aquatic forms; all Coelenterates live in water, and the great majority in the sea. One kind of Coelenterate, however, can often be found in ponds or streams in the summer in this country. This is Hydra, which is usually attached to water weeds. One species is green in colour and is about one-tenth of an inch long, while another species is brown and is rather larger. Hydra can sometimes be obtained by gathering water weed and placing it in a laboratory tank with some of the fresh water, and then waiting for the animals to appear on the glass.

Hydra is seen under the microscope to be made up of large numbers of cells, a characteristic which the Coelenterates share with all the other phyla of animals which we have still to study. The cells are arranged in two layers (see Fig. 41), separated by a thin layer of jelly-like material. In jellyfish this middle layer is enormously thickened, forming the bulk of the body. The cells enclose a central cavity with a single opening, the mouth. The ring of tentacles around the mouth has clusters of sting cells, which fire off in large numbers when a water flea or small worm brushes past. The struggling flea is pushed into the mouth by the tentacles and digested in the central cavity; any insoluble material must be removed via the mouth, since there is no other exit. As Hydra is small and all its cells are exposed to the water outside it or that in the cavity, it manages without special organs for respiration or excretion, and spends most of its time attached to one spot.

During the summer months, when the water contains lots of prey, Hydra grows rapidly to full size and then reproduces by a method called 'budding'. This is the outgrowth of the body to form a new individual (see Fig. 41), which eventually breaks free to live on its own. Budding is a form of *asexual reproduction*, since it does not involve the production of gametes, followed by fertilisation (if you do not remember clearly what is meant by these terms, look back at p. 47). Hydra does show *sexual reproduction*, usually in the autumn when prey is becoming scarce. Some individuals produce large numbers of male sex cells, sperms, while others develop one or more female sex cells, eggs. Both sperms and eggs may be formed on a single individual, although they do not usually ripen at the same time. When the sperms are ripe they are released into the water and one fertilises each egg. (Compare the process of sexual reproduction in a flowering plant, p. 47.) The fertilised egg develops a hard coat, and falls to the bottom of the pond where it can survive the winter, whereas the adults die.

Examination of seaweeds often reveals branched colonies made up of many connected hydra-like forms. Such a one is Obelia (see Fig. 42), the whole colony of which spreads over only a few inches. Corals live in similar, although larger, colonies, but produce deposits of calcium carbonate around themselves, sometimes in delicate or intricate forms, such as the organ-pipe coral, or in solid masses, like the brain coral.

We have already mentioned jellyfish and sea anemones; another interesting type of Coelenterate is the Portuguese man-o'-war. This floats in the surface waters of warmer parts of the Atlantic, with a bright blue sail sticking up to catch the wind. South-westerly winds in some summers blow shoals of them towards our shores. The long tentacles, which trail in the water, are used for killing fish for food and can inflict painful wounds.

All the forms of Coelenterates we have mentioned have the two layers of cells, separated by jelly material, the central cavity with only one opening, and the ring of tentacles with sting cells. A good way of following up your study of this group would be to gather more information on the subject of coral reefs, and the extraordinary variety of life which inhabits them.

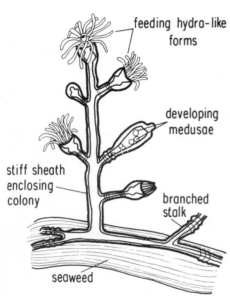

feeding hydra-like forms

developing medusae

stiff sheath enclosing colony

branched stalk

seaweed

Fig. 42   A small part of an Obelia colony on a seaweed. The Hydra-like forms catch minute animals for food. The colony buds off tiny medusae, resembling jellyfish, which are carried by ocean currents and produce eggs and sperm. A fertilised egg gives rise to a new colony

Fifteen

Worms and more worms

According to one dictionary, a 'worm' is a kind of invertebrate limbless creeping animal, although it can also mean an insignificant or downtrodden person, as well as a spiral part of a screw. The limbless creeping animal corresponds to what we think of as a worm, although it sometimes does have vertebrae, as in the case of the reptile called the slow-worm. Names like glow-worm and meal-worm illustrate other uses of this mental picture. (Do you know what kinds of animal these are?) When William Blake wrote

> *O Rose, thou art sick!*
> *The invisible worm,*
> *That flies in the night, . . .*

the only resemblance of this creature to, say, an earthworm was its shape!

Not so very many years ago biologists had a large group, called the Vermes, which means worms, into which were placed those animals fitting our original definition. A closer study of their internal structure revealed that the Vermes was rather a hotch-potch of three large phyla, plus some very small ones. The three major phyla are the Platyhelminths (flatworms), the Nematodes (roundworms) and the Annelids (segmented worms).

Platyhelminths

In many a pond or stream one can find small black or brown creatures gliding along over the bottom, over weeds, or even on the underside of the surface film. These are planarians, fresh-water Platyhelminths, and their long but flattened-from-above shape is characteristic of that phylum. Planarians (see Fig. 43) are attracted by a small piece of meat hung in the water, touching the bottom, by a length of cotton. When a number have collected on the meat it can be pulled out and placed in a laboratory tank for closer examination of these interesting creatures. Their gliding movement is always rather fascinating and is brought about by the beating of thousands of tiny hairs on the underside of the body. They can also swim, by rippling movements of the body.

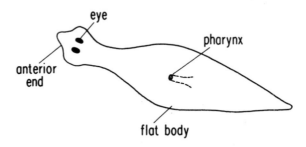

Fig. 43   A planarian

In nature they are scavengers, feeding on the bodies of dead water creatures, by means of a sucking tube, the pharynx, which can be pushed outside the body to suck off pieces of the food. If you can watch the planarians feeding, you will be surprised to find that the mouth is not at the front end, where one expects it to be, but more than halfway back along the underside. The mouth leads into a digestive system, branched extensively, but without any separate exit for indigestible matter, which must therefore pass out of the mouth. Planarians also have a system of tubes for getting rid of excretory waste, rather complicated reproductive organs, a nervous system, and sense organs which include eyes. In many of these respects, then, they are built on a more elaborate pattern than are the Coelenterates.

The free-living planarians form one of the three classes of Platyhelminths; the other classes, the flukes and the tapeworms, live as parasites on other animals. As an example we will take the pork tapeworm (Fig. 44). The long ribbon-like tapeworm lives in the intestine of a flesh-eating mammal, which could be a human, absorbing the digested food which is all around it. It hangs in position by means of suckers and hooks at its front end, called the scolex. This end continually produces new sections (proglottids) which contain reproductive organs. When the eggs have been fertilised and have

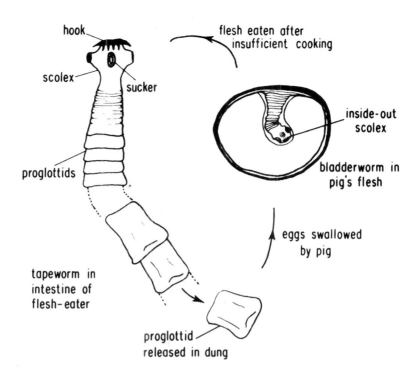

Fig. 44 A tapeworm life cycle, showing transfer from one host to another

formed shells, the ripe proglottids fall off and pass out of the mammal in the dung. If this dung happens to fall among grass or earth, some of the eggs may get swallowed by a pig rooting around for food. They hatch in the pig's intestine, giving a larval form which bores its way through into the flesh of the pig. Here it forms a bladder, so this stage is called the 'bladderworm', inside which grows an inside-out scolex. If the pig were now killed and eaten by a wild animal, or the meat eaten by humans without it being thoroughly cooked first, the tapeworm would be introduced into the intestine, and the life cycle would start all over again.

Because the tapeworm absorbs much of the mammal's food, a human being who is so unfortunate as to play host to one may become very thin, but is also likely to incur disorders brought about by poisonous substances given off by the worm. The parasite can be attacked by drugs which kill the scolex, so that it drops from the intestine wall and is passed out with the dung, but prevention is better than cure. The careful inspection of meat carcases by trained inspectors, so that meat containing bladderworms does not reach the shops, has made this parasite rare among people in Western countries. It remains all-too-common in countries where standards of food hygiene are low, and where large hunks of meat are often only partly-cooked over open fires.

Nematodes

In contrast to the flatworms as regards shape are the round-worms, but they are similar in the parasitic habit shown by almost all the Nematodes. As an example we will consider Ascaris, a roundworm common in pigs, which occasionally infects man (see Fig. 45). Ascaris lives in the intestine, eating some of the pig's food, but this loss is not serious unless there are many worms in the one pig. Fertilised eggs pass out with the dung and hatch in the soil, producing minute young worms which, if swallowed by another suitable host, will grow to adult size in its intestine. As in the case of the tape-worm, large numbers of eggs are produced, because many of the young fail to reach a suitable host.

Many roundworms have more complicated life histories than Ascaris, notably some of those which can live in man, with very harmful effects. Examples of these are hookworm,

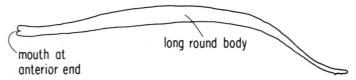

long round body

mouth at anterior end

Fig. 45 *Ascaris*, a roundworm. Note the·smooth surface, lacking external features. This is common among parasites which live inside the host

Filaria (the cause of a disease called elephantiasis) and guinea worm, all found in the tropics. Try to find out where in the body each of these lives, how it gets into a human, and what preventive measures can be taken.

A group of roundworms known as eelworms attack various plants and can be very destructive to crops, as is the potato-root eelworm. The eggs of this worm can survive in the soil for several years and, like those of other Nematodes, are very difficult to destroy. Therefore it is necessary for farmers to rotate their crops around various fields so as to avoid a rapid increase of the pests' numbers in any one field.

Annelids

These can be described as segmented worms, for the body shows a series of ring-like units. These are the segments. The segments are easily seen on an earthworm, a familiar member of this phylum. Actually, there are 37 different kinds of earthworm in the British Isles; the description given here is based on a large, deep-burrowing form called *Lumbricus terrestris*. This is the worm which drags dead leaves into the tops of its burrows. Like other earthworms, it swallows soil, digests the decaying matter inside the soil, and passes out the

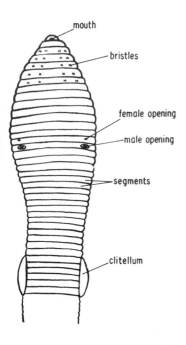

46 External features of an earthworm. Only the anterior end is shown, viewed from the underside

remainder. This species of earthworm is not one of those which leave worm casts of the passed-out soil on the surface.

Examine a preserved earthworm for external features (see Fig. 46). Look for the following:

1. The long tubular body.

2. The many similar segments.

3. At the front end is the mouth, on the underside of the first segment. A small lobe is in front of the mouth, but this is not a segment.

4. At the tip of the rear end is another opening, the anus, from which the soil is passed out of the body.

5. Look for tiny bristles on each segment. There are four pairs per segment.

6. If the worm is full-grown it will have a saddle of six thickened segments, the clitellum. This produces slime during mating, and also a bag of slime in which the eggs are laid.

7. Look for a small pair of openings on the underside of the 15th segment. These are the male openings, used in reproduction.

8. Segment 14 has on its underside the pair of very small female openings, through which eggs are laid.

Now you need to use a live worm, noticing first the moist skin through which the worm takes in oxygen for respiration. Allow the earthworm to crawl across newspaper. Look and listen. Can you see how the worm squeezes some parts of its body so that they become narrower and longer? This pushes the worm forwards. While it is happening, other parts of the body are anchored by means of the bristles. Paper does not give a good hold to the bristles, which drag across the paper, giving the rustling sound. Those parts of the worm which have pushed forward now become anchored while the rest of the body is drawn forward.

Although earthworms have no organs for respiration other than the moist skin, they do have a set of blood vessels for carrying oxygen and foodstuffs to all parts of the body. They also have a pair of excretory organs in each segment for the removal of dissolved wastes. The movements and activities of worms are controlled by a nervous system.

Earthworms often emerge from their burrows after dark, especially when the surface is damp. If you go out quietly at such a time you can find out whether they are sensitive to

touch – do this gently, with a blunt pencil or similar object;

light – shine a torch on the front end. Does the earthworm respond, although it has no eyes?

vibration – stamp on the ground nearby.

85

As do other animals, a worm must employ its senses in obtaining food, in finding a mate, and in avoiding animals which would eat it.

Some of the worms which have come partly out of their burrows may be found in the course of mating. Two worms lie side by side, enclosed in a layer of slime, with the head of each pointing towards the other's tail. A tiny drop of fluid comes from each animal's male openings and passes into the other worm's body. The fluid contains minute swimming sperm cells, the male gametes (do you remember the male gametes of a flower and those of Hydra? Sperm cells are the typical male gametes of animals). The sperm cells fertilise the eggs which are laid into a bag of slime produced by the clitellum and buried in the earth. Some time later tiny worms hatch out.

Many thousands of worms live in a single acre of good soil and their burrowing activities are of benefit to the farmer. Where worms have been at work more air can get into the soil, and surplus water drains away more easily. The swallowing of earth and the forming of worm casts helps to turn over the soil, encouraging the growth of plants.

A great many Annelid worms live in water, mainly in or on the sea-bottom. The ragworn and the lugworm used by sea anglers are Annelids which burrow in the sand or mud of the tidal zones. Leeches are Annelids which lack bristles, but have suckers. Many of them feed on blood which they suck from wounds they have made in the skin of other animals. We can be thankful that our climate is unsuitable for the leeches which hang in tropical forests waiting for a human or other mammal to pass by. Add to this the absence of the Nematode pests of tropical areas mentioned earlier in this chapter, and we may conclude that our often-despised weather has its advantages!

Sixteen

Animals in armour

Have you ever thought what it wo[uld]
armour? The men who made arm[our]
between making the metal plates [...]
spear, lance and sword thrusts an[d...]
soldier to move his arms and leg[s...]
armour were very cleverly made, [...]
wearer could have confidence in its [...]
move.

Well as they worked, the armou[r...]
far surpassed by the phylum of [...]
Arthropods have a strong skeleton [...]
encasing their bodies, a skeleton w[...]
dom of movement. The Arthropo[ds...]
successful in nature that about th[ree mil-]
lion or so known animal species b[...]

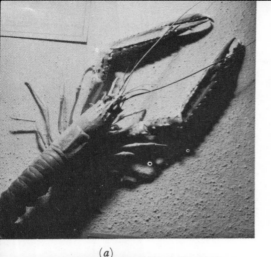

(a)

damp dark places such as under piles of garden litter or fallen timber. Examine a wood-louse to answer the following questions:

1. Has the animal a skeleton? Is it on the outside or the inside of the animal?

2. How many segments can you see?

3. How many legs are there? How are they arranged – singly or in pairs? The leg-bearing part is the thorax. Behind it is the abdomen with much shorter limbs.

4. Can you see joints on the legs? A joint is a place where a limb can be bent or straightened during use.

5. Note the eyes and the feelers on the head. In addition to the long pair of feelers, can you find a much shorter pair in front of them? The short pair are rather hard to see, but a hand lens will assist your search.

6. Under the head are jaws, difficult to see because of the small size, which are used to chew plant food, food that sometimes consists of a gardener's choice young seedlings.

The wood-louse belongs to one of the major divisions of the Arthropods, the class of the Crustaceans. It is unusual among Crustaceans in living on land, since almost all are aquatic. Crabs, lobsters, shrimps are marine Crustaceans of comparatively large size. Others of length less than an inch at the most live in countless numbers in the surface waters of the seas and provide food for fishes such as the herring.

In many of the large Crustaceans, as in a crab or lobster, the skeleton is very heavy – people often call it a 'shell' – and there is a large shield covering the upper surface of the head

Fig. 47   A.   Photographs of arthropods. (a) Lobster. (b) Locust. (c) Spider

(b)

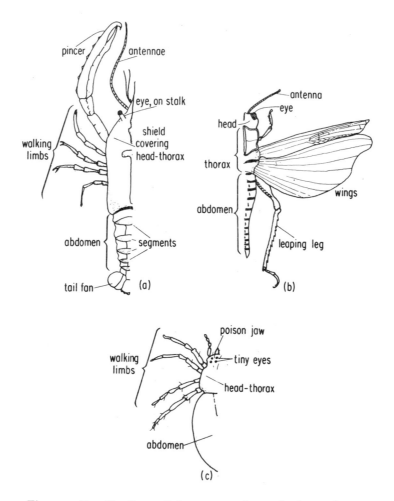

Fig. 47 B. Outlines of the same arthropods, from above

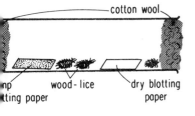

Fig. 48 An experiment
with wood-lice

and thorax. There are four pairs of walking limbs, just in front of which is a large pair of pincers used to grasp food or in self-defence (see Fig. 47). These water-living Crustaceans have attached to the upper parts of their legs gills, flat plates richly supplied with blood, where they take in oxygen from the water for their respiration. Wood-lice, living on land, use air-tubes for respiration instead of gills. However, they cannot survive in dry air for very long because they lose water vapour rather quickly through the thin skeleton and the air-tubes.

Experiment 28. Do wood-lice seek damp surroundings?

Collect a number of wood-lice; ten is about the minimum for a fair result. Place a strip of dampened blotting paper in one end of an open glass tube, and at the other end a similar strip of dry blotting paper (see Fig. 48). Introduce the animals,

89

close each end with a cotton-wool plug, and then gently move the tube to spread the animals along its length. Leave for 10 minutes. Do the wood-lice show preference for any region?

You could now go on to find out whether they avoid light. This time place damp blotting paper at both ends, but after putting in the animals cover one end of the tube to make it dark. Leave the other end exposed to light. Leave and observe as before.

Crustaceans, then, have in common with all other Arthropods a hard and complete external skeleton, a segmented body and pairs of jointed limbs. Most of them live in water and have gills for respiration, and in these respects, as in some others, they differ from other Arthropods such as Insects and Arachnids.

Insects

Insects are all around us. They intrude upon our attention again and again. Some because they are helpful, like the bees which pollinate the flowers of crop plants. Others please us less, for instance domestic nuisance the housefly, or the malaria-spreading mosquito. What other examples of helpful or harmful insects can you think of?

Insects as a group of animals have been tremendously successful in colonising all sorts of places, some as unlikely as one could possibly imagine. Inside a pod from a gorse bush you will very often find one or more tiny beetles of the kind known as weevils. Each has spent its life inside a single developing gorse seed, smaller than the head of a match. Various other insects are known to live in flour, cayenne pepper, and opium. The numerous orders of Insects include the following:

Common Name	Name of Order
Locusts and grasshoppers	*Orthoptera*
Dragonflies	*Odonata*
Earwigs	*Dermaptera*
Beetles	*Coleoptera*
Butterflies and moths	*Lepidoptera*
Flies, gnats and mosquitoes	*Diptera*
Bees, ants and wasps	*Hymenoptera*

Many of the biological names shown here end in 'ptera', meaning wings; '*Lepidoptera*' means scaly wings, while '*Diptera*' indicates two wings. The possession of wings is a characteristic feature of most adult insects, and insects are the only animals, apart from birds and bats, to have wings.

Most insects live on land, and those adults which inhabit freshwater, like the water boatman or the great diving beetle, show signs of having developed from land-living forms. Insects

...as to a sudden growth
...apid increase in locust
... the vegetation grows
... together. This is the
...ocusts. A vast swarm of
...ts out for new pastures,
... Great areas of Africa,
...e liable to suffer from
...al boundaries, so inter-
...ial in protecting crops.
...he numbers of locusts
in different areas, and watch for signs of swarms. When a swarm is noticed, it is attacked and destroyed by insecticides, which may be sprayed from aircraft, before serious damage can be done to vegetation.

In the locust, the young resemble the adult apart from the wings, but in many insects the egg hatches to give a form quite unlike the adult. This occurs, for instance, among beetles, flies, bees, butterflies and moths. In May, female large white butterflies lay eggs on cabbage leaves. The eggs hatch to give caterpillars. The caterpillar looks very different from the adult. It is also different in its movement and its feeding.

The adult flies about and uses its legs only for alighting on plants and when resting. The adult feeds on nectar which it sucks from flowers by using its long tongue. The caterpillar chews cabbage leaves with the aid of a pair of stout jaws, and moves by crawling. There is so much difference between caterpillar and adult that there is a special stage of life between them, the pupa. The caterpillar when full grown finds a tree or fence and turns into a resting stage which neither feeds nor moves. Inside the pupa the adult body forms and later breaks out to fly away. There are two generations of

5. Where is the mouth? The anus is harder to find, as it is hidden under the edge of the shell, as is the opening into the lung, an air-filled space. The walls of the lung are richly supplied with blood-vessels, and it is here that the snail obtains its oxygen for respiration.

6. Watch from the underside when the snail is moving over glass. Do you see rippling movements of the muscles in the foot?

7. Does a snail leave a trail? In moving it glides over a layer of slime which it has itself produced.

8. What is a snail's pace? Find the times taken to travel measured distances. An average of several trials is much better than only one result. Calculate your snail's speed as an hourly rate.

Snails belong to the phylum *Mollusca* – soft-bodied, unsegmented animals, many of which have a protective shell. The head of a Mollusc is not clearly separate from the body mass, and there is usually a fleshy foot.

Many snails live in freshwater (pond snail, Fig. 20) or the sea (whelk, Fig. 52); these types of Mollusc are called Gastropods (this means, literally, stomach-foot). While many Gastropods feed on plant food, some are flesh-eaters, such as the whelk. The whelk bores through the shell of an oyster and is then able to suck out the soft body. When the whelk itself is threatened by a larger animal, it is able to withdraw its foot into the shell, closing the opening with a hard, horny plate.

Another Gastropod which is well protected is the limpet, whose shell grows to fit very closely to a hollow in the rock where it lives. Although the limpet must crawl around to find the seaweed on which it feeds, it always returns to its own resting place. If it is attacked, the shell is pulled down against the rock and the animal uses its foot to hang on so firmly that it is very hard to pull off.

Slugs, on the other hand, are land Gastropods in which the shell is absent or small and hidden under the skin, so they usually hide under leaves or in the soil during daylight.

A second group of Molluscs consists of the Bivalves, which have two shells joined by a hinge. Mussels, cockles (see Fig. 52) and scallops are all Bivalves. Many of the shells one finds on the seashore are of Bivalves which live at the bottom of the shallow waters. Most of them plough very slowly through the mud by moving the fleshy foot, although scallops swim by flapping their two shells, while oysters and mussels do not move about at all in the adult stage. For most Bivalves, the only means of defence is that of using powerful muscles to hold the two shells tightly closed. Bivalves draw in a current of water through a tube called a siphon and pass it over large gills. The gills are used not only to obtain oxygen but also to filter off minute particles of food, which are then passed to the mouth.

The octopus and the squid are examples of the third major group of Molluscs, the Cephalopods, all of whom live in the sea. They have large eyes, and the foot extends around the head as a circle of arms or tentacles (see Fig. 52). These bear suckers which are used to grasp prey, such as crabs, which are

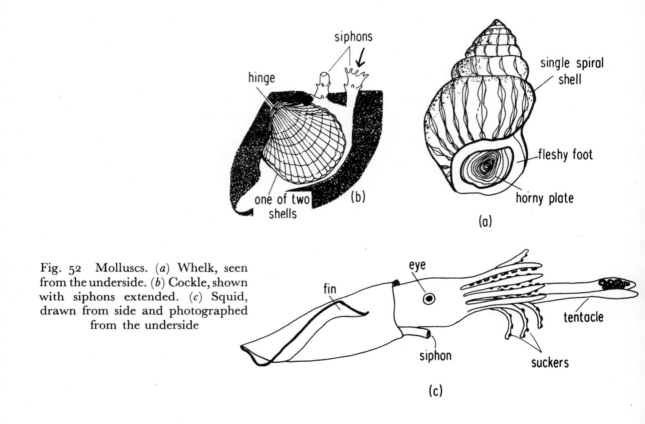

Fig. 52 Molluscs. (*a*) Whelk, seen from the underside. (*b*) Cockle, shown with siphons extended. (*c*) Squid, drawn from side and photographed from the underside

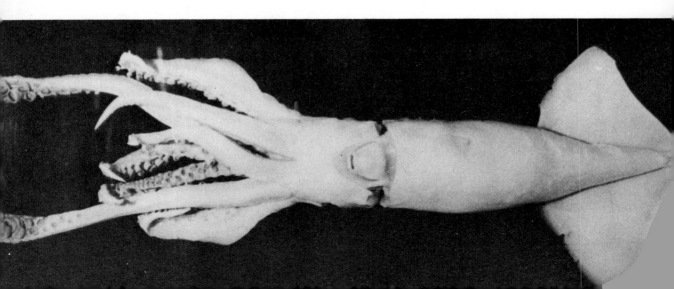

crushed by a horny beak before being swallowed. When a squid is alarmed it is able to change its colour very rapidly and repeatedly, and if this fails to mislead a pursuer, it can release a cloud of dark ink into the water. This confuses the enemy while the squid jet-propels itself quickly away, by squirting water out of its siphon. The siphon is the outlet tube for water which has been passed over the gills to provide oxygen for respiration. In some Cephalopods there is no shell, but in squids there is a plate of chalky material embedded in the flesh. This is sold as 'cuttlefish bone' for cage birds to peck.

Although not much is known about them, very large squids of perhaps up to 50-foot length inhabit the deep waters of the oceans. Sperm whales dive down to feed on them, and the marks of squid suckers have often been seen on the skin of captured sperm whales. Squids generally are very active creatures, with a way of life strikingly different to that of the slow-moving Molluscs.

Eighteen

Spiny-skinned animals

All the spiny-skinned animals, the Echinoderms (*Echino* – spiny; *derm* – skin) live in the sea. You will have seen some of them on the beach in the form of starfish and sea-urchins. Other kinds of Echinoderms are brittle-stars, sea-cucumbers, and sea-lilies (see Fig. 53 and Fig. 31).

All these animals have chalky plates embedded in their skin and bearing spines, although these plates are few and far between in sea-cucumbers. On the outside, too, and between the spines are soft finger-shaped projections, the skin-gills, used in respiration. The starfish, sea-lilies and brittle-stars all have a number of arms coming from a central disc-like portion, but there are no such arms in sea-urchins and sea-cucumbers. Echinoderms are unique in the animal kingdom in having a system of water-filled tubes which end in many tiny 'tube-feet'. The water in these canals is taken in through minute openings in the sieve plate (look at the starfish in Fig. 53), and can be forced into the tube-feet to extend them. A starfish, for instance, pulls itself along by extending some of its tube-feet, each of which then adheres to the sea bottom by its tiny sucker, while the animal pulls up the rest of its body to the feet. The process is repeated again and again, giving very slow progress, in which any one of the arms can be in the lead.

Starfish feed on oysters and other bivalve Molluscs, attaching their tube-feet to the shells and giving a steady pull until at long last the bivalve muscles tire and can no longer hold the shells shut. Then the starfish protrudes its stomach through its mouth, forces it into the gap between the shells, and digests

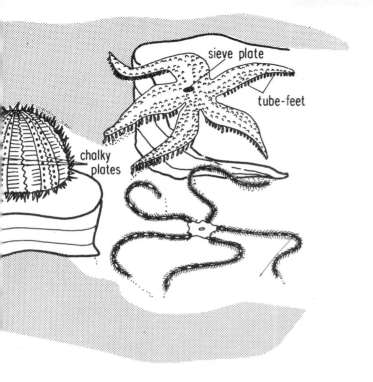
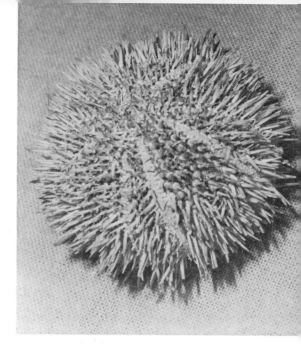

sieve plate

tube-feet

chalky plates

53   Echinoderms in a sea-bed ng. Left, sea urchin; top right, fish; bottom right, brittle star. photograph shows a dried skeleton of a sea urchin

away the unfortunate Mollusc's body. For this reason, starfish can do serious damage to oyster beds. At one time, fishermen who caught starfish in their nets cut them in halves and threw them overboard. This was a disastrous policy, since each half could survive and grow the missing parts!

Brittle-stars have a small button-like central disc and long thin arms, which are lashed to bring about movement. Underwater photographs of the English Channel near Plymouth have shown seething masses of brittle-stars covering the sea bottom, where they feed on small worms and Crustaceans.

Sea-lilies are permanently fixed (see Fig. 31) and are deep water forms, living at the upper end of a long jointed stalk. These arms spread widely and are used to sweep small organisms into the mouth.

Nineteen

Backboned animals

What have a fish, a frog and a man got in common? Not much, you might say! But you would be wrong. Although their external appearance is so different, there are some very important basic similarities. One of them is the possession of an internal skeleton, part of which takes the form of the backbone. This backbone is a row of separate bones, the vertebrae; hence the name Vertebrates, applied to all these animals.

In the very early stages of life, Vertebrates have a rod of gristle in the place where later the vertebrae form. This rod is called the notochord. Some odd marine creatures such as sea squirts (in their young stages), lancelets and acorn worms (see

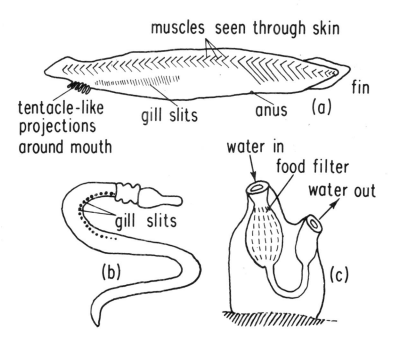

54 Chordates which have a [c]hord but no vertebrae. (*a*) Lan[celet.] This lies almost buried in the [sand] and uses its tentacles to sweep [food] particles into its mouth. It can [swim] in a fish-like way. (*b*) Acorn-[worm.] This burrows in the sea [botto]m and looks very worm-like. [(*c*) S]ea squirt. The egg hatches into [a ti]ny tadpole, with notochord, [whic]h swims for a time and then [settle]s on a rock and transforms into [a s]quirt. The squirt then filters off [food] particles from water which it [draws] in and then discharges – hence [the name]

Fig. 54) also have a notochord. So these, too, are classed with the Vertebrates in the phylum of the Chordates.

Fish

There are five classes of Vertebrates: fish, amphibians, reptiles, birds and mammals. Biologists believe that the fish were the first of the five classes to make an appearance in the history of life. We will give them our first attention. We need to examine a fish, but a fish will not stay alive for very long once removed from its home in the water. It will be easier to look at a preserved specimen first to identify some of the basic features. Do this with the aid of Fig. 55, and the following notes:

55 Photograph (*opposite*) and [v]iew of a bony fish. Only a few [of the] scales have been drawn

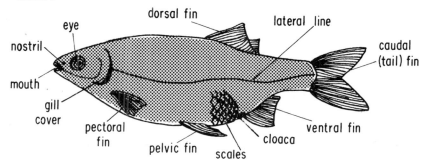

1. The body has a head, a trunk and a tail with a tail fin. Is there a neck?

2. Note the streamline shape, tapering towards each end. Has man imitated this shape in making structures to move easily through the water? What examples can you think of?

3. Note the scales, covered in slime, and overlapping. Does the unattached edge of a scale point forwards or backwards? Do you think this has any significance?

4. Look for the mouth, the pair of nostrils, and the two eyes. Are there any eyelids?

5. On the underside, more than halfway from the front end, is the cloaca – the single opening for wastes and for reproduction.

6. Examine the gill covers. Lift up the free edge of one gill cover to see underneath it the gills used to extract oxygen from the water.

7. Inspect the fins. Which of them are in pairs, which are single?

8. Can you see, about halfway down each side, a narrow line running from just behind the gill cover to the end of the tail? This is the lateral line, sensitive to disturbances in the water.

To get enough oxygen for respiration, a fish needs to pass a current of water over its gills. Watch a live fish in an aquarium tank. Where does water enter the fish, and where does it leave? Watch the mouth and the gill cover.

When the fish moves, see how it pushes against the water with the long tail part of its body. First the tail beats to one side and then to the other, and the push it gives against the water propels the body forward. Meanwhile, the fins help to keep it balanced.

Great numbers of kinds of fish exist, both in fresh and in salt water. Freshwater fish are all Bony fish, with a skeleton made of bone, and many marine fish such as cod and herring belong to this group. The females lay their eggs in the water, where they are fertilised by sperm cells from the males. The eggs are small and laid in large numbers, (a herring can lay as many as 50,000 in one spawning) but many are destroyed by other animals before they hatch. Most of the tiny fish, or 'fry' as they are often called, which do hatch are also eaten before they become full-grown, so the number of adults remains much the same over the years.

Sharks, skates, rays, and dogfish are Cartilaginous fish, having a skeleton made of cartilage (gristle). These all live in the sea. They have no gill covers, and their scales are pointed, not flat. The dogfish can be taken as an example of

Fig. 56 Mermaid's purse

their reproduction. The male passes its sperm cells into the female's body, and she lays eggs one at a time, each in a horny case. The case has tendrils which anchor it to seaweed (see Fig. 56) and it serves to protect the young fish until it has used all the food of the large yolk and can look after itself. The empty cases are often washed up on the beach and are called mermaid's purses.

The other classes of Vertebrates have two pairs of limbs, corresponding to the paired fins of a fish, and bearing a number of toes. Five is the full toe number, but many Tetrapod (four-legged) Vertebrates have fewer than this – a horse has

7 Amphibians. Toads (right) and a newt

only one toe on each foot. Many of these Vertebrates with legs are familiar to us as land animals of our own country.

Amphibians

This class includes the frogs, toads, and newts (see Fig. 57). Adult amphibians live on land and breathe by means of their soft, wet skin as well as their rather small lungs. They must keep to moist places so that the skin does not become dry, and must go to water to breed. The frogs pair in spring, at ponds and streams, and shed their soft eggs and the sperm cells into the water. The tadpoles which hatch from the eggs can swim by lashing the long tail and breathe by means of gills, while the adults have legs, no tail, and lungs. So great changes are

tadpole into the frog.

crocodiles are all reptiles
Fig. 58), while the dinosaurs
his class. Reptiles have scaly
ey need through their lungs.
yolks enclosed in hard shells,
the female's body before the
g is protected from drying or
o does not need to be laid in
h hatches from the egg re-
pable of land life.

on the names of examples,
athers, and their front limbs

Twenty

Algae and Fungi

Algae

Have you ever noticed a green powdery coating on old wooden gateposts or fences, or a tree trunk? If you look more closely you will find that it is not evenly spread around all sides, being much more abundant on the damper sides. In which compass direction do these sides face? Account for this being the damp side.

Scrape off a little dust and examine it under the microscope. Here is a tiny one-celled plant, called *Pleurococcus* (see Fig. 61). Can you see the characteristic features of plants – the cell wall, the chloroplasts containing the green chlorophyll, and the absence of structures for movement? Moisture and dust

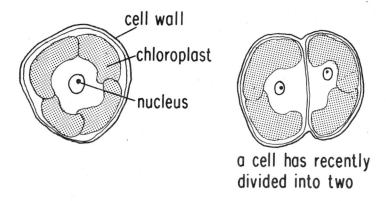

cell wall
chloroplast
nucleus

a cell has recently
divided into two

Fig. 61 *Pleurococcus*

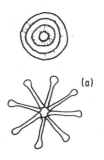

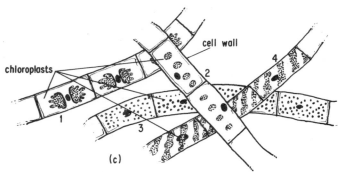

Fig. 62   Some Green algae: (*a*) Diatoms in which the protoplasm is inside a glass-like wall. (*b*) Desmids, which like diatoms are one-celled. (*c*) Blanketweeds, 1, *Zygnema*. 2, *Mougeotia*. 3, *Tribonema*. 4, *Spirogyra*

collect in the crevices of the wood on which the *Pleurococcus* is growing, and from this dust the plant obtains the mineral salt it needs.

Pleurococcus is classed as one of the Algae, a major phylum of the plant kingdom.* It is very unusual among the Algae in living on land and not in water. Many Algae are found in fresh water. Look for the masses of green threads which tangle around water plants, or float to the surface and form a green scum. Such Algae are often called blanketweeds. Examine a few threads, mounted in water, under the microscope. In each thread, can you see a number of cells? How are they arranged? There are several different Algae of the same general appearance, and you may be able to identify your material as one of those shown in Fig. 62.

Other kinds of fresh water Algae are the tiny desmids and diatoms (see Fig. 62 (*a*) and (*b*)) and you can expect to find some of these samples of pond water. Some can even thrive in the laboratory bottles of distilled water, getting the traces of salts they need from the glass of the bottle.

Another major group of Algae which you must have seen are the seaweeds. With only one or two exceptions the plants that live in the sea are Algae. You see lots of these on rocky coasts, on breakwaters or washed up on the beach. Among them are wracks, found in the tidal zones, and the oarweeds of deeper water (see Fig. 63). These seaweeds are brown in colour, while some others are red. This does not mean that they have no chlorophyll. Other pigments are present too and mask the green colour. The Sargasso Sea has mile upon mile of floating seaweeds of these kinds and the crews of sailing ships feared this area. The light winds and lack of strong currents could leave the ships becalmed for days, surrounded by masses of the weed.

Although some seaweeds reach considerable size they have

* Some biologists regard the Algae as a collection of several distinct phyla.

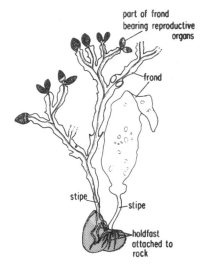

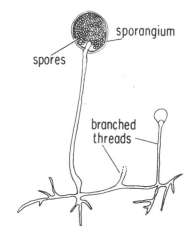

Fig. 63   Bladder wrack and oarweed.   Fig. 64   A mould fungus

no stems, roots, or leaves, and in this they are akin to the smaller Algae we have examined. The flatter parts of a wrack are known as the frond, and the stalk-like part, the stipe, connects to the holdfast which sticks to rock or timber. The frond bears, inside slight swellings, the reproductive organs. These produce eggs and swimming sperm cells, which are released into the water. After fertilisation has taken place the egg divides to give many cells and grows into a new plant.

The sea also contains many Algae of microscopic size, floating among the surface waters. Such Algae serve as food for many of the tiny animals which live alongside them in the plankton. (Plankton is the general name for all the surface life of small size, carried here and there in the ocean currents). In turn, the plant-eating plankton is eaten by larger animals and so on, up to the larger fishes which may be eaten by man. In recent years, certain Algae have been used as the source of various chemicals needed in making toothpaste or ice cream. The agar used in laboratory work with bacteria is extracted from seaweed.

Fungi

Experiment 29. To culture some mould Fungi on bread.

Moisten a piece of stale bread and leave it in a container with a loose lid for several days. Examine it for the growth of plants. If there are any, as is very likely, are they green plants with chlorophyll? If not, what colours are present? Damp bread usually becomes colonised by plants without chlorophyll called Fungi. We often refer to these sorts of Fungi as moulds. You will probably have seen some Fungi in your experiments with bacteria (page 76).

Use forceps to pull off a little of the fungus material, mount it in a drop of water, and examine under the microscope. Can you see a tangle of branched threads? This is the body of the fungus. From the mass of threads there grow upwards other threads which bear rounded heads. Each head is a sporangium full of minute round spores. Can you see these on your slide? (see Fig. 64). The spores get blown into the air and drift around. If a spore falls on suitable moist food it germinates and a new mould has begun its life.

Because Fungi have no chlorophyll they cannot make their food as green plants do. Instead they must use ready-made food, by giving out digestive fluids which turn the food into dissolved substances which are then absorbed into the fungus. In the case of the mould called mucor, bread is a suitable food, while for a mushroom it is dead matter in the soil. The part of a mushroom we see is the part that produces the spores. Long before the mushroom emerges from the soil its threads have been growing through the earth and absorbing food from decaying matter there. Other Fungi, such as many toadstools and puffballs, have similar habits.

Yeast is another interesting example of a fungus. Have you ever seen dough, to which yeast has been added, bubbling and heaving as the yeast makes it rise?

Experiment 30. To culture yeast.

Shake a little baker's yeast, or some dried yeast, with water and then add it to a solution of cane sugar in a flask with an outlet tube so that gas can escape. Leave in a warm place. Do you observe bubbles forming in the mixture? Allow some of the gas to pass into a tube of limewater. What happens? What is the gas? Now look at a drop of the mixture under the microscope. You should be able to see the small roundish cells of the yeast, some of them joined in chains (see Fig. 65).

Yeast breaks down sugar to obtain the energy it needs for its life and growth, and in doing so it can make alcohol as well as carbon dioxide gas. When yeast is used in bread making, the carbon dioxide makes the bread rise, but when the dough is heated in the oven the yeast is killed. In the making of

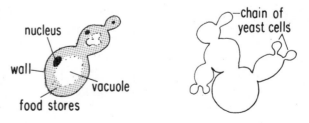

Fig. 65   Yeast cells. A chain is formed by budding from a single parent cell

wines, yeasts use the sugars in the grape juice and produce alcohol from them.

Some Fungi feed upon live plants or, in a few cases, on live animals. These Fungi are therefore parasites. Some parasitic Fungi do great damage to man's crops, as do the fungus diseases of wheat rust and potato blight. In both these cases, spores carried by wind settle on the plants and the fungal threads penetrate the stems and leaves. In feeding on the crop plant's cells the fungus grows at the expense of the wheat or the potato. Wheat rust does not kill the wheat plant, but causes a big reduction in the yield of grain. Potato blight can kill the potato plant and if it gets into the tubers it makes them unfit for eating.

Ringworm and athlete's foot are human diseases caused by Fungi which can live in our skin. Ringworm is most likely to be contracted by people who work with cattle, in which it is common, whereas the athlete's foot infection can be picked up by bare feet in places like changing-rooms. Thorough drying of the feet after a bath or shower is important in reducing the risk of picking up this fungus, since it needs moist places on the skin to start its growth.

To the biologist, the Fungi are of great interest because of the various ways in which they obtain their foods although they lack the chlorophyll of other plants. Many of the Fungi which live in the soil, feeding on the dead remains of plants and animals, are of great importance in nature. By the breakdown of such remains, their materials are released and return to the soil for the benefit of new generations of living things.

Our last mention of Fungi must concern Lichens, which can be found as grey or yellow patches on roof tiles or on rocks. Lichens consist of a tangle of fungal threads enclosing small single-celled green Algae. The fungal threads help to hold the Lichen in position and to trap water and salts, while the Algae carry out photosynthesis, so each helps the other. In the wintry climates of the near-Arctic regions few plants can survive, but there are many Lichens, and these provide food for the animals, including the reindeer.

Twenty One

Mosses and Ferns

What plants grow in little green clumps on roof tiles or on the tops of old walls? The answer is mosses. They are able to live in dry places, but must have water available for their reproduction. Pull one or two strands from such a clump of moss and examine with a hand lens or the low power of a microscope. Look for slender green stems with leaf-like outgrowths and at the base of the stem some hair-like structures used to absorb water and mineral salts (see Fig. 66).

At certain times of the year, moss plants bear a slender stalk with a swelling on the top. This swelling or capsule contains many tiny spores. Earlier still, the moss plants had produced male and female organs. The egg cells were fertilised by male sperm cells which had been released into rain water and had swum to the egg cells. After fertilisation the egg developed to form the capsule. If you look with a good hand lens at the tip of a ripe capsule you will see a ring of teeth which open when the weather is dry and release the spores. The spores blow about and if they land on a suitable place develop into new moss plants. We can sum up the life story of a moss like this:

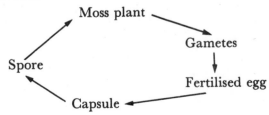

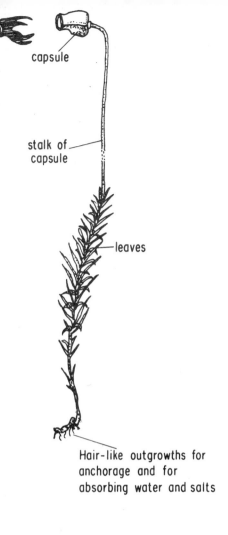

capsule

stalk of
capsule

leaves

Hair-like outgrowths for
anchorage and for
absorbing water and salts

Fig. 66   Common Polytrichum. The drawing shows a single stem, bearing a capsule from which the
cover seen in the photograph has been removed

Fig. 67   A liverwort (surface view). *Lunularia*, a weed on flowerpots in greenhouses, which reproduces
by means of buds developed in the crescent-shaped portions on the surface of the liverwort

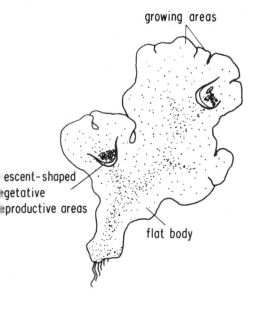

growing areas

escent-shaped
egetative
eproductive areas

flat body

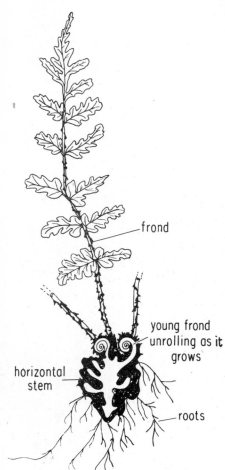

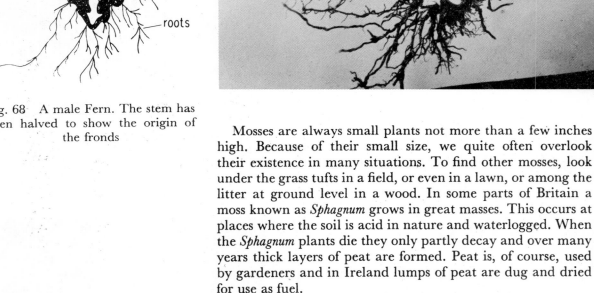

Fig. 68 A male Fern. The stem has been halved to show the origin of the fronds

Mosses are always small plants not more than a few inches high. Because of their small size, we quite often overlook their existence in many situations. To find other mosses, look under the grass tufts in a field, or even in a lawn, or among the litter at ground level in a wood. In some parts of Britain a moss known as *Sphagnum* grows in great masses. This occurs at places where the soil is acid in nature and waterlogged. When the *Sphagnum* plants die they only partly decay and over many years thick layers of peat are formed. Peat is, of course, used by gardeners and in Ireland lumps of peat are dug and dried for use as fuel.

Liverworts are classed together with mosses as the Bryophytes, but they are found only in damp shady places such as the edges of streams. A liverwort has a flat green body without shoots or leaves (see Fig. 67), but its method of reproduction is very similar to that of a moss.

Ferns

Ferns are much more conspicuous plants than mosses, although they are on the whole confined to damp and shady places. Many ferns live in woods. An exception to the general rule is bracken which grows in vast numbers in many parts of Britain where the soil is acid in nature. We find bracken, for instance, in open parts of the New Forest, on the Breckland of East Anglia, and on the slopes of hills in Northern England and Scotland. Bracken spreads rapidly by means of underground stems which grow horizontally through the soil and from which daughter plants arise. Some ferns are grown in shady corners of gardens, as is male fern (see Fig. 68), while maidenhair fern is a popular pot plant.

If you have a whole fern plant that you can examine, note that it has a stem (this may be horizontal rather than upright), roots and leaves. The leaves of ferns are usually called fronds. Your plant may have on the underside of the fronds little patches of dark powdery spore cases. When a spore case is ripe it slowly dries until it suddenly splits open, releasing the tiny spores. The spores blow about and if they fall on moist ground germinate. The germinating spore does not, however, produce a new fern plant. Instead a small green plate-like prothallus is formed, looking like a tiny liverwort. If you have ferns in a garden or a greenhouse, look underneath them for specimens of the prothallus stage; they will be small, less than a quarter inch in diameter. Bracken prothalli are sometimes found in the damper soil of the entrances to rabbit burrows. The prothallus produces gametes. The male gametes, the sperm cells, must swim in a film of water to reach the egg cells and fertilise them. A fertilised egg then develops into a new fern plant.

Here is a summary of the fern life story:

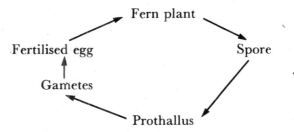

Mosses, liverworts, and ferns are all land plants but their life on land is limited by the need for surface water in which the male sperm cells can swim. Only a few kinds can survive anywhere except in damp places.

Twenty Two

The Seed Producers

The plants we have been discussing in the last chapter were producers of spores. As such they are of great interest to biologists, but all together they form only a minor part of the earth's land vegetation. The plant world as we usually think of it is the world of the seed-bearers. A seed is, as we saw in earlier chapters (Chapters 9 and 11), a special structure for dispersal of the species and for the survival of unfavourable conditions such as cold or lack of water. Its food stores enable it to survive for some years if necessary and then to spring into growth when conditions are right. The seed is a very important feature in the successful life on land of those plants which produce it.

The seed formers are called Spermatophytes (meaning, seedbearing plants). They all have roots, stems and leaves; the flowering plant we studied at an earlier stage (Chapter 4) serves us as a representative example. Our fields, hedges, gardens, lawns and woods are full of flowering plants in great variety. These are the Angiosperms, one of the two great divisions of the seed-bearers. Do you remember, from our studies in Chapter 8, that flowers contain ovaries, enclosed in which are the ovules that develop into seeds? All Angiosperms carry their ovules inside closed ovaries, with a stigma to catch the pollen needed for fertilisation.

Among Angiosperms we find small herbs, bushes and great trees, but they all produce flowers (see Fig. 69). The differences between the types of flowers that these plants bear are important in grouping them into the various families of Angio-

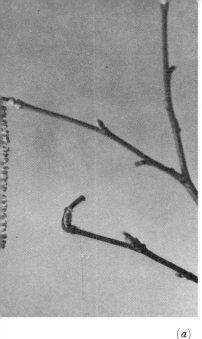

(a)

sperms. Just a few of the families with which we are most familiar are shown in Table 5.

Table 5. Some Families of Flowering Plants

English Name	Botanical Family Name	Some Examples
Buttercup family	*Ranunculaceae*	anemone, clematis, peony, marsh marigold
Rose family	*Rosaceae*	blackberry, strawberry, apple, peach, cherry
Wallflower family	*Cruciferae*	shepherd's purse, all kinds of cabbage, turnip, radish
Pea family	*Leguminosae*	Beans, clovers, laburnum, gorse
Daisy family	*Compositae*	dandelion, asters, chrysanthemum, sunflower
Grass family	*Gramineae*	all grasses, wheat, oats, maize

. 69 Some flowers of Angio-
rms. (a) Hazel catkin. (b) Daffo-
half flower. (c) Pear

Do you notice that these families include many of our farm and garden crops? Other families include familiar trees like oak, beech, horse-chestnut and so on. If, however, we lived in more northerly parts of Europe – Norway or Sweden, say, or in Canada, the great forests around us would not be of trees like these. They would be made up of cone-bearers, or conifers (see Fig. 70), which provide the material for the timber industries. When sawn into planks and beams they form softwood timbers for house-building and many other

Fig. 69   Some flowering plants

(b)   (c)

Fig. 70 Conifers. Note the almost bare earth under the trees; few plants grow in their shade

purposes. In warmer regions, conifers grow mainly on mountainsides, where the air is colder than at lower levels. Conifers can withstand the cold conditions better than the broad-leaved trees like oak, and so we often find a belt of conifers above the highest point at which the broad-leaved, deciduous trees (see page 53) are growing. In the last 40 years large numbers of conifers have been planted by the Forestry Commission in Wales, Scotland, Northern England and East Anglia. They grow in great plantations on soils which are poor for farming use, and contribute to our national timber needs.

Conifers are evergreen (larch is an exception, shedding its leaves in the autumn) and they have characteristic leaves, often called needles. Examine the needles of a pine tree. How

Fig. 71 Pine cones. The large one is a ripe female cone, while a cluster of tiny male cones can be seen at the tip of the branch

do they differ from those of a tree such as oak or horse-chestnut? Consider the overall shape, the texture, and the amount of wax on the outside. The special features of conifer needles considerably reduce the loss of water vapour from the leaf. This is of great importance in the cold climates which are the home of conifers, for when the soil is cold and sometimes frozen it is difficult for roots to obtain water.

Conifer means cone-bearer, and at some time or other no doubt you have handled one of the woody cones (see Fig. 71) that are found underneath such trees. Do you know what part it has played in the life-story of the tree? If you look closely at one of the projections (scales) on such a cone you will see on the upper surface two slight hollows. In each hollow there was a seed, and occasionally you can find one still there, although most have blown away. Now, these seeds are produced on the upper edge of the scale and they have never been enclosed in an ovary. Hence we can describe the parent as naked-seeded, which is what the name Gymnosperm means. Conifers are not the only Gymnosperms, but the other forms occur only very, very occasionally in this country and then always as planted garden specimens.

In its early stages the female cone is much smaller than it is when dry and ripe, and it is softer and green at the time when it is ready for pollination. This is brought about by wind-blown pollen, made inside small, soft and short-lasting male cones. When the male cones are ripe, they burst open and release clouds of tiny pollen grains, a few of which are successful in getting blown on to the openings of the ovules. Here each forms a pollen tube with male nuclei, similar to that of an Angiosperm, described in Chapter 8. Hence, in all the seed-producing plants there are no swimming sperm cells and fertilisation no longer requires a covering of water on the plants. In this way the seed-producers are better suited to life on land than any of the other plant groups.

We have taken a pine as an example of the conifers. Other well-known conifers are cedars, monkey puzzles, spruces (the Norway spruce is the one used as the Christmas tree) and the yew from whose wood the archers of England made their longbows. The use of conifers for timber has been mentioned above, but we must not fail to remark that the paper on which these words are written was made from softwood pulp.

Twenty Three

In the beginning

72 Fossils, collected by the
or; they are by no means rare
s! Photographs at two-thirds
ral size except (*b*) which is half
(*a*) Bivalve shell, about 5 million
s old. (*b*) Ammonite shell (a kind
Cephalopod), 150 million years
(*c*) Belemnite shell (another kind
ephalopod, with an internal skele-
, age uncertain as specimen was
d on Cromer beach. (*d*) Shark's
1, about 60 million years old

Have living things always taken the form in which we see them today? For many centuries this is what was generally believed. For as long as there had been life on Earth, so it seemed, the kinds of animals and plants we see now had been in existence. However, as people began to learn more about the earth, and to study its rocks, they found in some the remains of living things which had existed long ago. These are fossils, which take many forms.

Sometimes a fossil is a piece of hard skeleton more or less as it existed at the time when it was part of a living creature,

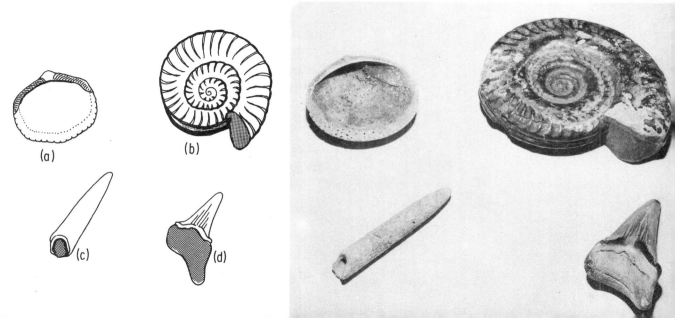

(a)　(b)　(c)　(d)

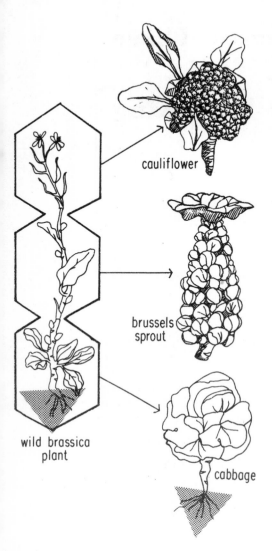

cauliflower

brussels
sprout

wild brassica
plant

cabbage

Fig. 73   Wild cabbage to vegetables

(see Fig. 72). More often, the original material has been 'petrified', turned to stone, but still shows the shapes and markings of its first state. Again, a fossil may be an impression, a footprint made in soft mud later turned to rock, or the outlines of a leaf or feather.

Now, the important point is that large numbers of fossils come from organisms not exactly like, and sometimes very unlike, those alive in the world today. As this was realised, so some thinkers began to accept the idea that the first-created living organisms must have undergone change to produce our modern forms. This point of view received support from the ways in which man's domestic animals and cultivated plants had been developed from originally wild forms. The heavy carthorse and the swift racehorse are both descendants of the wild horse, just as the cauliflowers, cabbages and Brussels sprouts of our gardens have been developed from a coast-living wild cabbage (Fig. 73). If man could obtain such differences by breeding from a common ancestor over a period of at most a few hundred years, could not much wider variation arise in the vastly longer times of earth history? In the early years of the nineteenth century, a French scientist named Lamarck stated that living things could undergo change, and that such change had occurred throughout the history of life. This is what we term *evolution*. However, he was not able to produce convincing evidence to support his ideas, and his theories as to how such changes could occur proved unacceptable, so few people took much notice of his writings.

The key point in our present understanding can be dated a few years later, in 1831, when a young Englishman, Charles Darwin, set sail as naturalist with the H.M.S. Beagle. This was a survey ship, sailing to chart coastlines and water depths at many places on a round-the-world journey lasting 3 years. Darwin's official duties were the identifying and recording of rock samples collected during the voyage. The ship sailed westwards across the Atlantic and then slowly southwards along the eastern coast of South America. Soon Darwin was filling piles of notebooks with his careful observations.

He saw that as the ship moved southwards, the species living in particular places were replaced by different, though similar, species. A striking instance of such difference was that between the Mammals of the North and South America. Even when living in similar conditions, the South American species were not the same as, and in some ways appeared to be less highly-developed than, their counterparts from North America.

In the pampas, or great plains, of South America the rivers cut through rocks which contain many fossils. Darwin saw a variety of fossil bones in the river banks, and some he was able to study closely. They included the remains of large mammals,

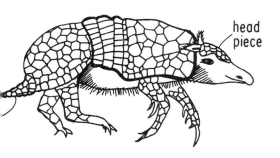

head
piece

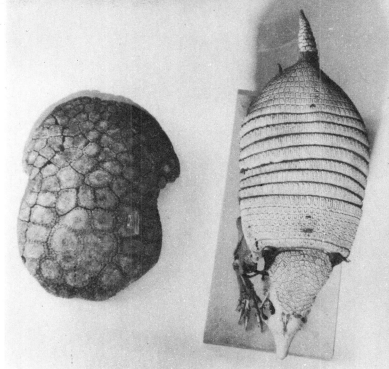

Fig. 74 Armadillo and Glyptodon. Top left, a modern armadillo. Top right, an armadillo skeleton beside the fossil headpiece of a glyptodon. Below, the massive tail of the same glyptodon, about one-fifth natural size

of types no longer in existence. Some had great plates of armour, like those of modern armadillos, apart from their size (see Fig. 74), while others were the bones of giant sloths far larger than the South American sloths of today.

Later the Beagle reached the isolated Galapagos Islands, separated by 600 miles of sea from the west coast of South America. Here he found that there were many unique species of organism, known nowhere else, but resembling forms found on the mainland. There were several kinds of finches, clearly related to, but yet different from, those of South America (see Fig. 75). There were even differences from one island to another, especially between the more distant islands in this scattered group. The animal inhabitants also included giant tortoises, and the islanders could tell by looking at the shell from which island a specimen had been taken. It appeared that each kind had been able, in the isolation imposed by the surrounding sea, to develop its own particular features.

After his return to England, Darwin spent many years working out his ideas on *The Origin of Species*, as his most famous book is titled, and collecting a great mass of supporting evidence. When, in 1858, he was still hesitating from publishing his work he received an essay from another naturalist who was at that time in Malaya, Alfred Russel Wallace. Wallace had spent 4 years in the forests of the Amazon, collecting specimens from the marvellous variety of life there, and in 1854 he began a spell of 8 years in the islands of Malaya and

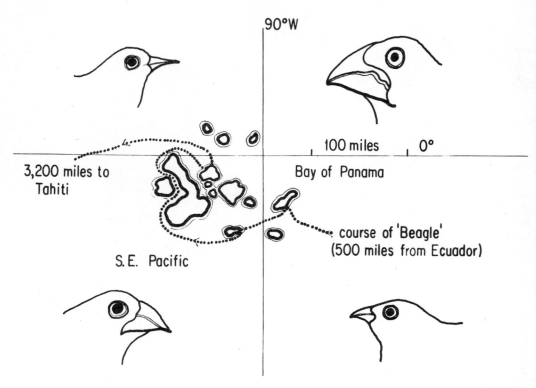

Fig. 75   The Galapagos Islands and four sub-orders of finch discovered on the islands

Indonesia. During this time he travelled 14,000 miles and collected over 125,000 specimens. In 1855 he had published an article in which he argued that modern species had developed from previously existing ones. His essay of 1858 went further, providing an answer to his own question, 'why do some members of a species die, and some live?' When Darwin read Wallace's essay, he felt that he must withdraw his own book, now nearly complete, in favour of Wallace, whose ideas had proved to be very much like his own, although without the wealth of supporting evidence Darwin had assembled.

Friends of both men helped to find an honourable solution, by way of a joint paper read to a meeting of the Linnaean Society of London on July 1st 1858. This was followed in 1859 by the publication of *The Origin of Species*. Great storms of argument were aroused, but eventually Darwin's ideas became an accepted part of biologists' thinking. Starting from the principle that evolution had occurred, Darwin argued that it had taken place as a result of *natural selection*.

All living things produce more eggs, seeds, or offspring than would be needed simply to maintain numbers at the present level. Darwin noted that the elephant is the slowest breeder among animals, and might produce 6 young in a lifetime of

100 years. Even so, in 750 years, one original pair could give rise to 19 million living descendants.

Not all of the offspring will survive to the age at which they can themselves breed. An oyster is reckoned to lay about 16 million eggs in its lifetime, but the number of oysters does not increase noticeably. Offspring are subject to many losses, especially in their early stages of growth, so that the numbers of a species remain much the same. Darwin observed a piece of ground, 3 feet by 2 feet, which had been dug and cleared, and on which 357 seedlings of native weeds appeared. Of these, no less than 295 were destroyed by being eaten, mainly by insects and slugs.

There is, in fact, competition for survival – competition between the members of a species, and between them and rival species, for light or food or shelter – a *struggle for existence*. In the struggle for existence, some individuals will have a better chance of survival than others. This is so because the members of a species show *variation* – some can run faster, or grow more quickly, or are better protected, or more efficient in the getting of food, than others. To use Wallace's own words, 'from the effects of disease the most healthy escaped; from the enemies the strongest, the swiftest, or the most cunning; from famine, the best hunters.'

The peppered moth, a woodland species, occurs in two forms, one a light buff colour, the other almost black. In woods well away from city smoke, the black forms show up clearly against the lichen-coated bark of trees, and are much more likely to be eaten than the light-coloured ones. Where city or industrial smoke blackens the trees and prevents the growth of lichens, it is the black form which blends with the background, the light form which is conspicuous and heavily preyed-on.

Some variations, then, confer an advantage on the individuals which possess them, and these ones have a better chance of surviving to breeding age. There will be *natural selection*, with *survival of the fittest*. Offspring tend to resemble their parents, so the following generations can maintain, and indeed by further change may improve on, the ability of the species to survive in its surroundings. At the time of Darwin little was known about the way in which offspring inherited characters from their parents. The scientific study of inheritance, known as genetics, is very much a modern development, and has enabled us to understand how the features of offspring are related to those of their parents. This is however a difficult subject, and we shall not consider it further at present.

It follows from the theory of evolution that the most advanced animals and plants have arisen from simple, less highly

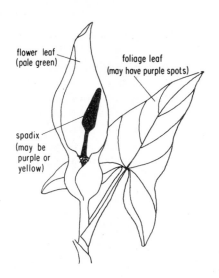

Fig. 76   The Cuckoo Pint

Fig. 77   H.M.S. *Beagle* in the
Straits of Magellan

developed ones. A very great many of the more primitive forms have become extinct, not being able to survive in competition with more advanced rivals, and we know them only as fossils. However, many have managed to survive where their way of life has not clashed with that of more advanced kinds. Hence we can find such a great variety of life in the world around us. Coelenterate and vertebrate, moss and spermatophyte, each form adapted to its own place and way of life.

Evolution takes place very slowly – it has taken hundreds of millions of years for life to take on its present forms – so it is not easy to see it happening around us. The case of the peppered moth is an illustration of natural selection going on at the present time. The cuckoo pint is a good example of a wild plant which shows clear examples of variation, although at present we do not know of any particular significance in the variations. Some plants have left coiling, and others right coiling, of the flower leaf (see Fig. 76). The spadix may be purple, yellow, or an intermediate colour. Some plants have purple spots on the leaves, others have none.

When the theory of evolution was set forth, there were many people who felt that it was destroying belief in a Creator who had made all things in the beginning. Is this really so? By way of answer, let us look at a passage which Darwin wrote in the conclusion to *The Origin of Species*:

'There is grandeur in this view of life, with its several powers, having been originally breathed by the Creator into a few forms or into one; and that, whilst this planet has gone cycling on according to the fixed law of gravity, from so simple a beginning endless forms most beautiful and most wonderful have been, and are being evolved.'

Figure 77 is a portrayal of another passage of Darwin's, one which shows us the importance of the theme of evolution to the study of biology. 'When we no longer look at an organic being as a savage looks at a ship, as something wholly beyond his comprehension; when we regard every production of nature as one which has had a long history; when we contemplate every complex structure and instinct as the summing up of many contrivances each useful to its possessor, in the same way as any great mechanical invention is the summing up of the labour, the experience, the reason, and even the blunders of numerous workmen; when we thus view each organic being, how much more interesting – I speak from experience – does the study of natural history become!'

Twenty Four

Life in a community — the hedgerow

In Mediaeval times, when most of Britain's population lived in small villages, the village land was worked on a system which gave one of the three huge fields a rest each year. Thus each plot of ground bore crops for two years out of three, and in the third year lay rough, grazed by animals to manure it. Each field was divided into many separate strips, some owned by each of the freemen, but there were no fences or hedges to divide one man's property from his neighbour's. In any event, a man's land was not all in one place, but scattered here and there. As Britain's population grew, particularly in the industrial centres, the old methods could not provide sufficient food.

During the 18th and early 19th centuries, the powerful squires and large landowners in almost all the villages were allowed to get Acts of Parliament passed whereby they could 'enclose' the village lands into farm fields under their ownership. Although great hardship was caused to the poorer villagers, the large fields they made were easier to cultivate and, with increased knowledge of cropping methods, were able to produce much more food than the old system.

It was at this time that a very great many hedges were planted, as barriers which would keep in the farm animals, as living fences. Often the hedge was planted on a raised bank, sometimes with a drainage ditch at the side. One of the most common bushes used to form the hedge was hawthorn, which grows rapidly, and makes a thick thorny mass difficult for animals to push through. Every few years the hedge would be

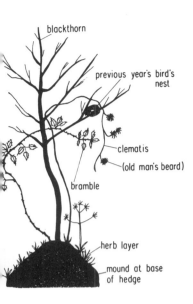

blackthorn

previous year's bird's nest

clematis

(old man's beard)

bramble

herb layer

mound at base of hedge

78 A hedgerow with a main structure of blackthorn, over which scrambles blackberry. The picture is taken in late winter, but many blackberry leaves are still hanging on. Many stems of clematis climb among the branches and overhang at the edges and still show a few clusters of feathery fruits which merit the plant's other name, old man's beard. Hedge parsley is the most numerous of the overwintering herbaceous plants at the hedge base, which is on a bank of soil at the roadside

trimmed, and often in doing this the stems would be partly cut through and then interwoven to give an even stronger framework. However, such hedges did not remain in their original state for very long. A wide variety of both plants and animals found ideal homes in the hedge or the bank underneath. So it is that the biologist can make a fascinating study of the life of a hedgerow, and the way its living organisms form a community, depending on one another for food or shelter or support.

We cannot study a hedgerow, any more than other kinds of living communities, from books; you will need to find a good example of a field hedge (not a neat garden hedge!) which you can visit at intervals. Unless you live in a large city, this

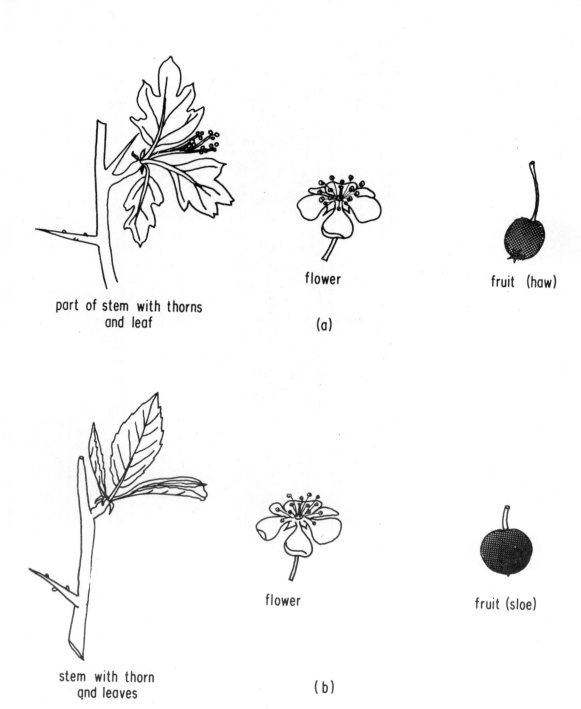

part of stem with thorns
and leaf

flower

(a)

fruit (haw)

stem with thorn
and leaves

flower

(b)

fruit (sloe)

Fig. 79 (*a*) Hawthorn. (*b*) Blackthorn

should not be too difficult; Fig. 78 shows a hedge just outside a city boundary. First, note its general features – the approximate height, thickness and length of the section you will study, the direction in which the hedge runs, and whether or not it is standing on a bank or accompanied by a ditch.

The height and thickness of the hedge will determine the amount of light which filters through to smaller plants. The direction of the hedge is important for if it runs North to South then both sides will receive about equal light; if it runs East–West then one side will be much more shaded than the other. If there is a ditch, then the hedgerow plants will overlap with those whose home is the damp soil of the ditch.

Identify the shrubs which are present, using the following information to help you, and note which are the main contributors to the bush layer of your hedge.

Hawthorn (see Fig. 79) has leaves with lobes and toothed edges; many of its short shoots end in thorns; its flowers appear in May, have white petals, and are followed by the red fruits, the haws. The bark is rather pale, and country people sometimes call it whitethorn to distinguish it from blackthorn. It is very common indeed.

Blackthorn has blackish twigs, and also bears short side shoots ending in thorns; the leaves are of simple shape and appear after the white flowers. The fruits are pea-sized plums, the sloes, of purple colour and very sour taste.

Sometimes other shrubs take their place as the backbone of the hedge, and one could make a long list of those that might be found. Examples are privet (found, apart from the form used in garden hedges, growing wild on chalky soils), elderberry, elm (usually growing from suckers developed from the roots of elm trees), dogwood, buckthorn, and wayfaring tree. A few of the more common are shown in Fig. 80, but for fuller details one can consult some of the numerous guides on trees and shrubs, e.g. *Trees and Bushes in Wood and Hedgerow*, by Vedel and Lange, published by Methuen.

When a hedge has been left to grow unchecked for two or three years, there is a good opportunity for the growth of a second group of plants. These make use of the sturdy bushes to provide support for their own weak stems. They are the climbing or scrambling plants, equipped with various devices which will enable them to hang on to the bushes. If you see on a hedge something that looks rather like a marrow or cucumber plant, it will be white bryony. Each year soft green shoots grow quickly upwards from ground level, and cling to the shrub stems by means of long sensitive tendrils. Before a tendril comes into contact with a stem it is almost straight. You can find tendrils in this state near the tip of the shoot; work back down the shoot and find out what happens to these

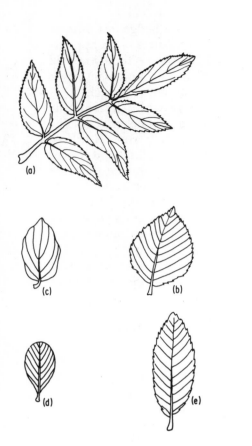

Fig. 80 Leaves of some hedgerow shrubs. (a) Elder. (b) Elm.
(c) Dogwood. (d) Buckthorn. (e) Wayfaring tree. All about one-
third natural size

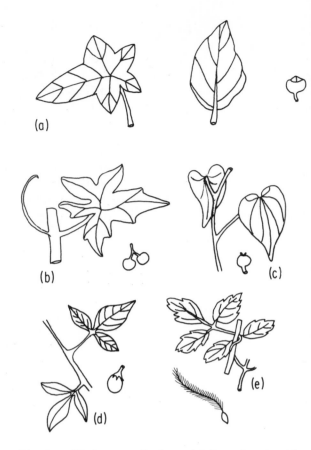

Fig. 81 Hedgerow climbers. (a) Ivy, showing the
usual foliage leaf (left) a leaf from a flowering
shoot (centre) and the berry, which is black when
ripe in October. (b) White bryony, leaf and tendril;
berries red when ripe in July–October. (c) Black
bryony; the berry ripens in September and is pale
red. (d) Woody nightshade; the berry is bright red
or black and ripe ones occur in July–October.
(e) Old man's beard, or clematis, or traveller's joy.
The dry fruits with the long hairy style are ripe in
autumn. All drawings are about half natural size

tendrils after they touch a stem. Try the effect of stroking one
side of a young tendril with the tip of a pencil.

Other climbing plants commonly found are black bryony
(quite unrelated to white bryony), old man's beard or traveller's joy (found on chalky soils), bindweed, woody nightshade
and ivy (see Fig. 81). If any of these are present in your hedge,
find out how they obtain support. If it is possible to do so,
scrape earth away to have a look at the root system of some

climbers. Particularly interesting are the ones which survive winter underground, as do the two bryonys and also bindweed. Black bryony is a member of the yam family of plants. Yams have thick fleshy underground tubers, which are used as food in the tropics. Has black bryony any similar structures? While we are discussing black bryony it may be appropriate to mention here that its fruits (and other parts) are poisonous, as are those of some other hedgerow plants like woody nightshade and cuckoo pint. Never attempt to eat such fruits, however appealing, until you have made sure that it is safe to do so!

Scramblers do not have such definite anchorage to the hedge shrubs, but bear projecting hooks which give them a hold. Examples of these are blackberry, wild rose (this in time will form quite strong stems of its own) and goosegrass (found mainly on the lower parts of the hedge). Look for these plants and for their hooks. Where do they occur on the plant, and which way do they point? What advantage is there in this? What happens if you attempt to pull a scrambler downwards?

Next we turn our attention to the plants which we find under, or at the bottom of, the hedgerow. Some of these are quite tall, perhaps reaching 2–3 feet. Among them are often Jack-by-the-hedge, stinging nettle, and hedge parsley. They are perennial plants which survive the winter (Do you remember how? Refer back to Chapter 11) and then make rapid growth in spring. This enables them to offset the effects of the hedge's shade by growing into areas of adequate light. Do their stems show any tendency to grow outwards from the bushes?

While we must not lose sight of our main purpose by going off into a consideration of water life, it is worth referring again to the hedge-side ditch. If your hedge has one of these, the tall plants mentioned will be accompanied by others which prefer damp waterside soils. Such are great willowherb, meadowsweet, and water figwort. Each of these is capable of producing stems 3–4 feet high in one season, and so they too grow up into zones of good light.

By the time that the tall plants have grown up, the hedge shrubs will be clothed in leaves and only poor light will reach the area around the bases of the bushes. Not many plants are capable of surviving here, but there are some which can thrive in the poor light. Among them we may number violets, cuckoo pint, primroses (in some parts of the country), and a number of species of moss. The first three have their main period of growth and flowering early in the year, before the full green of the hedge above has developed.

Now is the time to consider whether there is any difference in the plant populations on different sides of the hedge. If a photographic light meter is available you can compare the light intensities. Take care to make your measurements at equal distances from the hedge centre, and what sky conditions are similar. Are there any differences in the types or numbers of tall or shade plants which can be related to the differences in light intensity? To provide a satisfactory answer to this question you may have to take some sample counts, say of the number of plants of each kind in a yard of hedge length.

Differences in the amount of light, and so warmth, will affect the amount of water loss from leaves. This can be tested by the use of cobalt chloride papers. These are made by dipping filter paper in strong cobalt chloride solution and then drying it thoroughly. This paper is bright blue when dry but on exposure to moist air quickly turns pink. Keep your paper dry in a closed container until needed, then expose pieces of it, pinned to sticks, at similar places on each side of the hedge. Some might, for instance, be inside the bush layer, others at various heights and distances outside it. Take the time required for the paper to reach a shade of pink matching a standard dampened piece. Since plants differ in the rate of water loss they can stand (primroses, for instance, quickly wilt in sunlight), rates of water loss may also be important in accounting for the observed differences in plant distribution.

Spring and summer see the flowering and then the fruiting of the various plants we have found. Leaf and flower and fruit all provide food, or shelter, or both for many of the hedgerow animals. This is another side to life in a community, and one which we shall follow up in our next chapter.

Twenty Five

Living things depend on one another

At the time when we looked at the hedgerow in winter (refer to Chapter 11), many of the animals we found were in an inactive state. Some, such as earwigs, were overwintering as adults, but others were immature forms, for instance the privet hawk moth pupa. Now that we are studying the hedgerow in its summer greenery, how much more varied the active animal life is! Few animals are going through a resting stage, and those that are will not stay in it for long.

The small tortoiseshell butterfly occurs widely in Britain. It overwinters in sheltered places – often in crevices of buildings – as an adult, emerges from hiding around May, and the female lays eggs on stinging nettles. The adult has wings which are patterned with bright orange and black, with small patches of bright blue along the outer edge, on the upper surface. The underside of the wings is a dull, dusty black. The caterpillars are found in clusters on the nettles, and are about an inch long at full size. They are yellowish, with black speckles, and many short hairs. The black is particularly developed in a stripe down the back and one along each side. The young caterpillars spin silk with which they construct a tent of several nettle leaves drawn together. (Two other butterfly caterpillars also feed on nettles, those of the peacock, which are black with white dots, and those of the red admiral, which are black with scarlet spots.) The pupa of the small tortoiseshell is grey-brown, often with an old-gold tint, and can be found hanging upside down from a nettle leaf or the stem of a bush. This is a short resting stage, only a few weeks, and from it emerges an adult. The females of this new generation lay more eggs, it being now July, and the adults derived from these eggs are the ones which hibernate.

The meadow brown butterfly, whose caterpillars spend the winter hidden at the bases of the grasses on which they feed, is another example of an animal with a short inactive stage in summer. This again is the pupa, formed in May or June, and from which emerges the smoky brown adult seen flitting around the hedgerow from July to September. However, most of the animal inhabitants of our hedge will be very active in the summer months, and will reach their greatest numbers then. Winter is a time when there are many casualties, but the survivors breed and numbers build up again during the warmer months.

The small tortoiseshell illustrates for us two main ways in which animals make use of a hedge. The caterpillars feed on the nettle leaves, while the adults suck nectar from the flowers of the bushes and herbs. Secondly, the pupae obtain shelter during this helpless stage. The need for food and for shelter or hiding place are two main reasons why many of the animals are found around the hedgerow. Others may be visiting it in connection with reproduction – seeking a mate, or collecting nesting materials, as does the leaf-cutter bee, or to lay eggs, as the lackey moth does on bushes.

Careful observation during the summer months will reveal a great range of animal life, some probably well-known to you, but others to identify which you will need to consult guide-books. Our earlier work on the major groups of animals should give you a useful start to identification, and in those chapters a number of further references have been given. Your observations, recorded in a notebook at the time they are made, will also enable you to determine what biological needs brought the animal to the hedge. If it has come in search of food, there are several main ways in which this might be obtained:

By chewing plant stems or leaves
By sucking sap from young shoots
By eating fruits or seeds
By sucking nectar
By capturing animal prey

Consider the animals, called predators, which feed upon other animals, their prey. One predator will, in the course of a season, consume many individuals of its prey. A web-making spider, for instance, may catch and eat several small insects a day. This can only go on if there are far more of the prey than of the predators. There must, in fact, be a surplus left

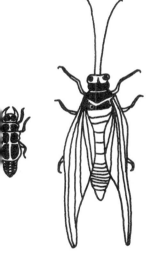

Fig. 82 Animals in a food chain. The greenfly are sucking sap from a primrose leaf (top left). The lacewing larva (bottom left) feeds on greenfly but the adult (bottom right) is often the victim of the spider (top right)

over after all the attacks of predators, as well as losses from other causes – accident, disease, winter cold, and so on – to breed and replenish the numbers of the species. Many preyed-on animals breed rapidly and produce great numbers of offspring – have you found any examples of this? If the numbers of predators become too great, they will bring about a reduction in the amount of prey available, and then some predators will starve or breed less freely. In time, the balance of numbers is restored, because fewer predators will mean more prey surviving, and so on.

Where did the prey get *their* food supplies? They might have preyed upon still smaller animals. A web-spinning spider might catch a lacewing fly which had itself used greenfly as food (these animals are illustrated in Fig. 82). If we trace back step-by-step, we soon come to animals which take plant matter as their food source. Because green plants are the only organisms capable of producing food from simple materials in the soil and the air, they must be the base of any such series. The greenfly makes use of them when it sucks sap from a plant shoot, and in this instance we can now construct a food chain:

Rose bush → Greenfly → Lacewing fly → Diadem spider

While many food chains in nature are very elaborate, with a large number of links, we should certainly find it possible to construct several chains from what we have observed about our hedgerow animals. In doing so we shall probably also see something of the decrease in population size as we go from one animal to the next in the chain, what is often called the *pyramid of numbers* (see Fig. 83).

Suppose that plants were to go on taking carbon dioxide, water and salts, and making them into the complex materials of their bodies, and that animals were to go on eating them as food, but nothing was returned to the soil or the air. Soon the supplies of raw materials would become exhausted, and all life would grind to a complete halt. This does not happen,

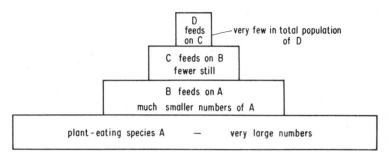

Fig. 83   Pyramid of numbers

because there are ways in which what has been taken from soil and air is returned.

Much of the water a plant absorbs is lost by evaporation from the leaves – hence the tests with cobalt chloride paper (Chapter 24) – and forms part of the water vapour in the air. Later it will return to the earth in rain. Some of the food which animals eat is lost from their bodies in wastes, such as dung and urine, while the respiration of all living things returns carbon dioxide to the air. In autumn, the ground is coated with the dead leaves of the hedge plants, and among them are the bodies of many dead animals. All such remains undergo decay, brought about by the activity of fungi and bacteria, and as a result their substances return to the soil, restoring its salts. By the spring the supplies in the soil will have been made good, ready to support another season of growth.

Living organisms which use decaying materials as a food source are known as aprophytes. Look for these in the hedgerow in the form of toadstools. Do any of these have the green pigment chlorophyll? Another decay Fungus to look for is one called *Nectria*, which occurs as small, bright pink patches on dead twigs lying on the ground. There are many others!

Another way of life is that of the organisms which we describe as parasites, organisms which live at the expense of a living host, which can be either a plant or an animal (refer back to Chapter 15). Hedgehogs are notorious for the crop of fleas and lice they carry. Contrary to what some people think, hedgehogs can scratch themselves, and I have often seen them doing so. However, fleas have very flat bodies which enable them to scramble quickly through the mass of spines to escape from the scratching. Lice are another kind of small insect which are like fleas in having needlelike mouthparts enabling them to pierce the hedgehog's skin and obtain blood as food. The amount consumed is quite small, and so there is little harmful effect on the host.

Greenfly can be regarded as parasites of plants, sucking the sap, but not killing the host unless their numbers become excessively large. Many fungus species are parasites of green plants. If you find orange or brown powdery patches on the leaves of hedgerow bushes, these will be the spore-forming areas of parasitic fungi living inside the leaves at the expense of the cells.

In all these ways, then, the living things of the hedgerow are seen as a community, depending on one another, and all upon the green plants which can use the sun's energy in making food. Each organism has its own particular place, to which it has become fully adapted in the course of evolution. Man, a highly specialised member of the successful mammal group, has made the hedgerow community possible, and goes on exerting a great influence on it. He affects it whenever he trims or lays the bushes, or cuts down the plants around the edges, or allows his chemical sprays and insecticides to drift over from the fields. He may even remove the hedge altogether to enlarge his fields in the interests of easier mechanical agriculture. Let him take care, so that such an act is not part of a greater destruction of the living communities on which all life, including ours, depends.

Twenty Six

Man and Nature

The first men on Earth were hunters, feeding upon animals they had caught with the aid of simple tools of stone, wood and bone. They also gathered fruits, seeds and edible roots from wild plants. Sometimes they were successful and fed well; at others, no doubt, they went hungry. As the centuries passed, not only did they improve their weapons, but slowly they learned to maintain herds and flocks. They began to practise the art of growing plants which would give a crop that could be stored for later use. Hunters had become herdsmen and farmers.

As agriculture improved, although extremely slowly, it became unnecessary for everyone to devote his time to collecting or producing food. Some men could spend their time on tool making and other crafts and exchange the things they made for supplies of food. Nevertheless, human populations for long remained small and scattered, and most of the earth's surface was untouched by human activity. Populations were limited by food supply, especially in lands with a cold winter, and by diseases such as smallpox, cholera, and bubonic plague.

The great advances in medicine and in public health measures such as sanitation, pure water supply and refuse disposal, which have taken place in the last hundred years have reduced death among infants and young children in the more prosperous countries to only a tiny fraction of their former proportions. This means many more mouths to feed, and also more living room, as seen in the mushroom-like growth of towns. As towns and villages grow larger, more and more acreage around them is used for houses, shops, factories and roads, and less remains for agriculture. To some extent this is compensated for by the increased production possible with modern crop varieties and livestock breeds, and the use of efficient farm machinery. However, there is also a pressure on untouched countryside, to bring it into cultivation. Such problems affect all countries, but they can be clearly seen in Britain, where a large and mainly town-dwelling population inhabits a not very big island. More and more areas of wild countryside are cleared or drained for farming or forestry, and only tiny patches here and there remain for the wild life which occupied them.

Man, then, by his occupation of an area tends to drive out many of its original inhabitants, both animal and plant, but this is not the only destructive effect that he exerts. Wild communities contain a mixture of plant and animal species, but for ease of cultivation and harvesting a farmer fills a field with plants all of the same kind, or keeps in it a herd of one species. In so doing he provides ideal opportunities for some other living organisms. These are the various pests and diseases which attack the particular crop plant or animal, and which can spread rapidly with so much food at hand. We can see this happening in our own home gardens, as for instance with the blackfly (aphid) pest of broad beans. Once a few of these sap-sucking insects have arrived on a single plant, they quickly give birth to more. (Do you remember Experiment 2, p. 8?) In a few days thick clusters are to be found on the soft stem tips and in a week or two the whole plant is affected. Badly attacked plants become sickly and the crop is largely spoiled.

Similar effects can occur in field crops – examples in Britain being the sugar beet aphid, which also spreads a virus disease among the crop, and potato root eelworm, a tiny Nematode worm which destroys the fine roots. Seed-eating birds, notably wood pigeons, often flock to a newly-sown field of corn and eat many of the grains before they have even germinated. House sparrows often collect in large flocks in cornfields to feed on the ripening ears, so reducing the yield.

To defend his crops against such ravages, the farmer calls upon the aid of scientists who produce chemicals capable of destroying the pests or disease agents. Many of these chemicals are very effective, but their efficiency has further consequencies. Many pesticides are fatal not only to the pest they are used to kill, but to other harmless and sometimes beneficial animals. D.D.T. is well known as an agent for killing unwanted insects, but if spray falls on water containing fish, these may die too. Large numbers of hive bees have been destroyed by insecticides sprayed on fruit trees around blossom time to kill insects which would damage the fruit. In other cases the chemical may kill a pest's natural predators, and so remove the natural checks on the pest's increase. Since 1955 the British populations of the peregrine falcon have declined rapidly, and there are grounds for connecting this and the use of certain insecticides of the organo-chlorine group. Peregrines feed on other birds, some of them seed-eaters which may have fed on seed protected from insect pests by these insecticides. The chemicals persist in the birds' bodies and then appear to accumulate in the peregrines, lowering their breeding power so they produce fewer young. Here is the operation of a food-chain with a vengeance!

Other ways in which we as a species adversely affect other species are the pollution of water by industrial waste or effluents – it's a long time since salmon came up the Thames past London Bridge! – the smoke and grime from our chimneys, and the fumes and carbon monoxide from our vehicle exhausts. Even the apparently harmless practice of picking and collecting specimens has its dangers. The Victorians had at one time a craze for marine aquaria, and Gosse, whose writings about rock pools had set it off, came to regret his words when he saw such pools stripped bare. Hosts of bluebell and primrose pickers have unwittingly contributed to their loss from many woods and hedgerows. Collectors of butterflies and birds' eggs have often speeded the decline of an already rare species by their eagerness to get specimens. In recent years the osprey began to breed again in Scotland, at first only one pair, and in spite of a guard kept on the nest, an egg thief managed to reach and steal the eggs, only to smash them during his escape.

This, then, is the black side of man's relationship with other species. What can we find to say on the other side? Although Man destroys many wild communities, he does provide some new homes for wild life. The reservoirs built for town water supplies, flooded gravel pits, and the dams of hydroelectric plants provide new homes which soon develop populations of aquatic life. Many wading and swimming birds are attracted to them, as they are to sewage farms, especially in winter time. The development of parks, and the planting of trees in town streets, also provide new havens for some kinds of animals, while tall blocks of flats in cities are being used as roosts and nesting sites for hawks and owls. I live in a town, but my moderate-sized garden receives a number of bird and mammal visitors:

Regular:	Occasional or Seasonal:
House sparrow	Bullfinch
Blackbird	Goldfinch
Song thrush	Feral pigeon
Robin	Rook

Chaffinch	Redwing
Blue tit	Mole
Great tit	House mouse
Starling	Long-tailed field mouse
Tawny owl	Hedgehog
Greenfinch	

If you are a town dweller, can you match this list from your own observations? You'll be surprised!

In the present century, many countries have set up nature reserves in which wild life is protected from hunting and other destructive human activity. Examples are the Game Parks of East and South Africa, and the National Parks of the U.S.A., great expanses of the countryside where the wild animals can roam freely. In Britain, Nature Reserves are smaller, but none the less important. The National Trust owns such reserves as Brownsea Island in Poole Harbour, with its sea-walled bird sanctuary, and Wicken Fen, in Cambridgeshire. At Wicken an area of marshy peat, such as made up the great belt (some 2,500 square miles) of East Anglian fenland, is preserved by pumping in water from the surrounding dykes. Rare fen plants such as the marsh sedge (*Cladium mariscus*) and the beautiful marsh pea survive there, as do the animals which feed on them, while elsewhere the draining of the fens has led to their disappearance.

Many local organisations, such as County Naturalists' Trusts, have purchased woods, ponds or heaths of especial biological interest for preservation as Nature Reserves. Cambridgeshire Naturalists' Trust owns Hayley Wood, a 120-acre fragment of oak wood, on heavy clay soil, much of which is believed to have been woodland continuously since the time when oak wood covered most of England. The preservation of such areas is not by itself sufficient. We need other measures too if the rest of our countryside is not to be deprived of much of its wild life. A step in the right direction was the restriction of the use of some of the more destructive and long-lasting pesticides, particularly of the organo-chlorine kinds. Further scientific research should lead to the discovery of pesticides which are less widespread in their effects, so that they do not destroy other species, or remain active in the soil for long after use. Better understanding of the proper use, and the dangers of misuse, on the part of farmers and others who handle chemical sprays is also needed.

Our attitude must be that of conservation. How much poorer the world of sight and sound would be without the wonders of nature! Many delightful living creatures have already disappeared completely because of the thoughtlessness or greed of man, the great auk, the dodo, and the passenger pigeon among them, and many others are even now on the verge of extinction. The World Wildlife Fund is helping to save some of the most dangerously threatened species, but the same attitude of preservation is needed if we are to keep many species which we now regard as common. If our study of biology so far has helped us to appreciate some of the intricate wonders of life in nature's communities, then we must make it our business to help preserve them for our own and future generations. What the National Trust booklet says about the care of Wicken Fen can be given a wider application. 'And so we ask our neighbours to take a pride in Wicken and to help us to preserve for the whole Nation the plant and animal treasures it contains – living things of perpetual beauty and interest which once lost can never be regained'.

index